ARTHUR C. CLARKE

Rendezvous with Rama

Retold by Elizabeth Walker

INTERMEDIATE LEVEL

Founding Editor: John Milne

The Macmillan Readers provide a choice of enjoyable reading materials for learners of English. The series is published at six levels – Starter, Beginner, Elementary, Pre-Intermediate, Intermediate and Upper.

Level control
Information, structure and vocabulary are controlled to suit the students' ability at each level.

The number of words at each level:

Starter	about 300 basic words
Beginner	about 600 basic words
Elementary	about 1100 basic words
Pre-Intermediate	about 1400 basic words
Intermediate	about 1600 basic words
Upper	about 2200 basic words

Vocabulary
Some difficult words and phrases in this book are important for understanding the story. Some of these words are explained in the story and some are shown in the pictures. From Pre-Intermediate level upwards, words are marked with a number like this: ...³. These words are explained in the Glossary at the end of the book.

Contents

A Note About the Author   4
A Note About This Story   6
The People in This Story   11

1 Project Spaceguard   13
2 Rendezvous With Rama   18
3 Into the Darkness   25
4 Up or Down?   31
5 Storm Warning   40
6 Light!   46
7 The Fears of the Hermians   53
8 New York   58
9 *Dragonfly*'s Flight   63
10 The Fields of Rama   68
11 Spiders   75
12 The Committee   79
13 The Hermians Make Their Own Plans   83
14 Rodrigo's Mission   87
15 The Temple of Glass   91
16 The Vast Space Beyond the Solar System   97

Points for Understanding   101
Glossary   105

A Note About the Author

Arthur Charles Clarke was born on 16th December, 1917, in Minehead, a town in the southwest of England. When he was nineteen years old, he moved to London where he became interested in studying astronautics – the science of travelling through space. He joined the British Interplanetary Society and he also started to write science fiction stories.

During the Second World War (1939–1945) Arthur C. Clarke was an officer in the British Royal Air Force. He worked in a department that was developing radar. This new invention found out the positions of the enemy's ships and planes.

After the war, Arthur returned to work at the British Interplanetery Society. He later became president of this society.

In 1945, he published a technical paper called 'Extra-terrestrial Relays'. It describes his ideas for communications instruments called satellites, which would remain at a fixed height above the surface of the Earth as they travelled on an orbit[1] around it. His invention brought him many awards and made him famous. Today the fixed orbit at 42,000 kilometres above the Earth is named 'The Clarke Orbit'. In 1948 Arthur C. Clarke obtained a first class degree[2] in Physics[3] and Mathematics from King's College, London. As well as studying science, Arthur Clarke continued to write science fiction stories and his first story, *Rescue Party*, was published in 1946.

In June 1953, he married Marilyn Mayfield, an American, but they separated in December 1953.

Arthur C. Clarke first visited Colombo, Sri Lanka, in December 1954. At the time, the country was called Ceylon. He became interested in diving underwater and he studied the plants and animals that lived in the ocean. He went to live in Colombo in 1956 and has lived there ever since.

In 1964, he worked with the American film director, Stanley

Kubrick. They wrote a science fiction film together. Four years later, he and Stanley Kubrick received an award nomination from the U.S. Academy of Motion Picture Arts and Sciences for the film *2001: A Space Odyssey*.

Arthur C. Clarke is one of the most famous and respected science fiction writers of the twentieth and twenty-first centuries. More than 50 million copies of his books have been sold all over the world. He has won very many awards for his writing.

His bestsellers include: *The Sands of Mars* (1951); *Childhood's End* (1953); *2001: A Space Odyssey* (1968); *Rendezvous With Rama* (1973); *The Fountains of Paradise* (1979); *2010: Odyssey Two* (1982); *The Songs of Distant Earth* (1986); *2061: Odyssey Three* (1987); *Rama II* (1989); *The Garden of Rama* (1991) (with the writer, Gentry Lee); *The Hammer of God* (1993); *Rama Revealed* (1993) (also with Gentry Lee) and *3001: The Final Odyssey* (1997). He has written many short stories. Among them are: *Tales of Ten Worlds* (1962); *The Wind From the Sun* (1972) and *The Sentinel* (1983). He has also written a large number of scientific papers and essays and non-fiction books. Arthur C. Clarke was the presenter of the very popular TV series: *Arthur C. Clarke's Mysterious World* (1981) and *Arthur C. Clarke's World of Strange Powers* (1984). He worked with famous American TV news broadcasters during NASA's Apollo 11, 12 and 15 space missions[4]. He is a member of the International Academy of Astronautics, the Royal Astronomical Society and many other scientific organisations.

On 26th May, 2000 in his home in Sri Lanka, he received a knighthood during a special ceremony. Sir Arthur C. Clarke continues to write and he uses phones, faxes and the Internet to discuss science fiction, astronomy, space travel and astronautic technology with his many friends all over the world.

A Note About This Story

[1 billion = one thousand million (1,000,000,000)]

Our **Solar System** began about 4.6 billion years ago. The Solar System – the word solar means of the Sun – was formed from a cloud of dust and gas which started to contract[5] and get hotter and hotter. As the cloud became smaller, the inside became dense and heavy because gravity pulled the outer layers inward. Gravity is an invisible power called a force. This force attracts things – it pulls them together. Gravity affects every object in the Solar System.

The pressure inside the cloud of gas and dust increased over a long period of time – maybe a million years. Then the heat, which was trapped by the gases, exploded. These enormous explosions made the material spin[6] round and round. Then this hot material contracted and the star at the centre of our Solar System – the **SUN** – was born.

The Sun is an enormous ball of glowing gas. The temperature at its centre is over 15 million degrees Centigrade. The temperature on the surface is 5,500°C.

After the enormous explosions which made the Sun, the material which orbited around it became planets and asteroids[7]. These planets do not stay at exactly the same distance from the Sun all the time. Each planet has its own orbit and each planet is a different distance from the Sun. Each planet's orbit has an oval shape – like an egg. It is not a perfect circle. Also, each planet rotates – spins round and round – as it moves along its orbit.

The length of a planet's 'day' is the time it takes to rotate one turn on its axis[8].

The Sun and all the stars that we can see in the dark sky are

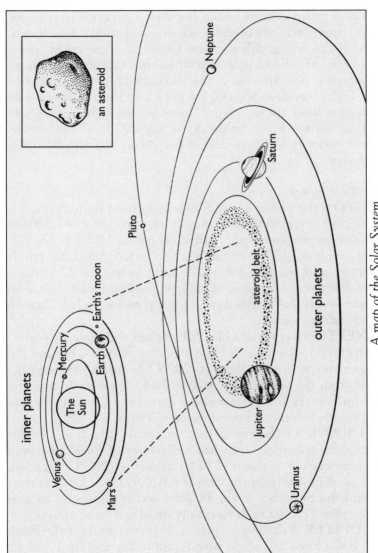

A map of the Solar System

part of a group of stars which is called a galaxy. Galaxies are huge – many billions of miles across – and they rotate slowly. Light is the fastest thing in the Universe, so scientists use a measurement called a light year when they talk about distances in galaxies. A light year is the distance light travels in one year. Light travels at 300,000 km per second and it travels 9.46 million million km in a year. Therefore one light year is 9.46 million million km. Our galaxy is 100,000 light years wide. The distance from the middle of our galaxy to Earth is 30,000 light years.

Our Solar System

PLUTO is the planet which is usually furthest from the Sun. It is the coldest and smallest planet. It has a diameter of 2,300 km and the temperature on its surface is minus 230°C (–230°C). Pluto's average distance from the Sun is 5,900,000,000 km. It orbits around the Sun every 248 Earth years. For 20 of these years, Pluto is inside the orbit of Neptune. Pluto rotates once on its axis every 6.4 Earth days. It has a moon called **Charon** which orbits around it.

   NEPTUNE is a bright blue ball of gases and there are powerful storms on its surface. It has a diameter of 49,100 km and the temperature above its clouds is –200°C. Neptune's average distance from the sun is 4,497,070,000 km. It orbits around the Sun once every 165 years and it rotates on its axis once every 16.1 hours. Neptune's largest moon is **Triton**.

   URANUS rolls around the Sun on its side. It is a bright blue-green colour. Uranus has a diameter of 51,300 km and the temperature at the tops of its clouds is –200°C. Uranus's average distance from the Sun is 2,870,991,000 km. It orbits around the Sun once every 84 years and it rotates on its axis once every 17.2 hours. It has many small moons around it.

   JUPITER is the largest planet. It is one-tenth of the Sun's size. It is a huge ball of gas with liquid in the middle. It has 16 moons circling around it. The largest of these are **Io, Europa, Ganymede** and **Calisto**. Jupiter has a diameter of 142,800 km and its surface temperature is –130°C at the tops of the clouds. Jupiter's average distance from the Sun is 778,833,000 km. It orbits around the Sun once every 11.86 years. It rotates on its axis once every 9.9 hours.

EARTH is the watery planet – two thirds of its surface is covered in water. From space, Earth looks blue, green and white. The atmosphere around the planet is made up of nitrogen, oxygen and a small amount of other gases. The warmth from the Sun keeps most of the water on the Earth as a liquid. The water at the North and South poles is frozen into ice. Water and an atmosphere are needed before life can exist. Earth has a diameter of 12,756 km and the temperature on its surface is on average 15°C. Earth has one moon, which is called **Luna** in this story. Earth's average distance from the sun is 149,597,900 km. It orbits around the Sun once in 365.2 days. This is an Earth year. It rotates on its axis once every 23.9 hours.

SATURN is the second largest planet and has a set of beautiful rings around it. These are formed from many small pieces of ice which orbit around the planet, many miles above it's surface. Saturn has many moons and **Titan**, the largest, has an atmosphere of nitrogen gas. Saturn has a diameter of 120,600 km and the temperature at the tops of its clouds is –185°C. Saturn's average distance from the Sun is 1,426,978,000 km. It orbits around the Sun once every 29.46 years and it rotates on its axis once every 10.7 hours.

MARS is cold and covered in red dust made from iron. Because of this dust, Mars is often called the Red Planet. It is only half the size of Earth. At each pole there is a layer of thick ice made from water and carbon-dioxide. There are also deep grooves[9] on the planet's surface. These grooves have no water in them now, but scientists believe that they were made by water millions of years ago. The diameter of Mars is 6,787 km and the surface temperature is on average −50°C. The Red Planet's average distance from the Sun is 227,900,000 km. It orbits around the Sun once every 687 days and spins on its axis once every 24.6 days.

VENUS is the same size as Earth and the surface is covered in thick clouds. The temperature on the surface is hot (480°C). The pressure on its surface is nearly one hundred times greater than on Earth. Venus has a diameter of 21,100 km. It's average distance from the Sun is 108,208,900 km. Every 225 days it travels once around the Sun. It rotates on its axis once every 243 days.

MERCURY is the planet which is closest to the Sun. There is almost no air on this planet. Mercury's average distance from the Sun is 57,909,100 km. It has a diameter of 4,880 km and a surface temperature of 430°C on the side facing the Sun, and −180°C on the dark side, away from the Sun. It rotates on its axis once every 59 days and it orbits around the Sun once every 88 days.

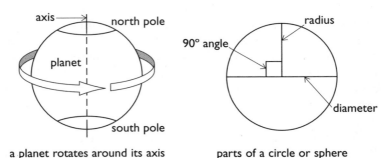

a planet rotates around its axis   parts of a circle or sphere

The People in This Story

Commander William Tsien Norton – captain of spaceship *Endeavour*. Age: 54. Born 2077 in Brisbane, Oceania, Earth. He has a wife on Earth and three children.

Lieutenant Joe Calvert – crewmember of spaceship *Endeavour*. Best friend of Karl Mercer. Calvert has a wife on Earth and one child.

Lieutenant-Commander Karl Mercer – second officer of spaceship *Endeavour*. Best friend of Joe Calvert. Mercer has a wife on Earth and one child.

Technical Sergeant Willard Myron – crewmember of spaceship *Endeavour*. He is a very clever mechanic.

 **Surgeon Commander Laura Ernst** – doctor on spaceship *Endeavour*

Lieutenant Boris Rodrigo

Lieutenant James (Jimmy) **Pak**

Sergeant Ruby Barnes

Sergeant Pieter Rousseau

Members of the Rama Committee:

Professor Olaf Davidson	– astronomer[10]
Dr Thelma Price	– archeologist[11]
Dr Carlisle Perera	– biologist[12]
Dennis Solomons	– historian
Conrad Taylor	– anthropologist[13]
Sir Lewis Sands	– historian of science
Dr Bose	– Chairman and Ambassador[14] for Mars
Sir Robert Mackay	– Ambassador for Earth
The Ambassador for Mercury	

1

Project Spaceguard

Earth and its people have always been in danger from deep space[15]. Millions of years ago, before there were men and women on Earth, meteorites[16] often fell on the planet. Some scientists believe that one of the biggest of these rocks caused the slow extinction[17] of the dinosaurs.

Long after the dinosaurs were extinct, humans developed on the Earth. And at first, humans were more fortunate than the dinosaurs. Meteorites did fall on the Earth sometimes, but they did little harm. They fell into the sea, or onto the land far away from people and their cities.

However, by the end of the twenty-first century, people were crowded together all over the surface of the planet. There were no more uninhabited spaces on Earth. Its millions of people lived anywhere that they could.

On a morning of September, in the year 2077, a huge ball of fire appeared in the sky over Europe. In a few seconds, the fireball – a huge meteorite – was brighter than the Sun.

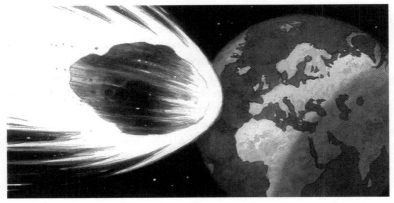

Then, without any warning, the meteorite began to break up in the sky above Austria. Crash after crash – each crash louder than thunder – terrified the people below. Soon, the sky above Europe was full of dust and smoke. The pieces of the meteorite fell to Earth, moving at 50 kilometres a second.

A thousand tonnes of rock and metal smashed onto the plain[18] of northern Italy. Soon, the water of the Adriatic Sea had risen to cover the city of Venice forever. Six hundred thousand people died when that meteorite hit the Earth. In Italy, the art and architecture of many centuries was destroyed in a few minutes. The shock to Earth and its people was terrible.

After this shock, all the people of Earth decided to work together. If they wanted to guard their planet against dangers from space, they had to work together. As a result of this decision, war between countries came to an end. From that time, the military and scientific knowledge of the planet was used to protect people, not to destroy them. Project Spaceguard was developed, and from that time its scientists watched the sky. If danger came again from space, the people of Earth would be ready for it. They believed that they could protect themselves.

———

Danger did come again – in the year 2131. Long before that date, humans had been living beyond the Earth. There were people living on several of the planets in the Solar System – Mercury and Mars, as well as Earth. There were also people living on Luna – the Earth's moon – and on Ganymede, Titan and Triton, three of the larger moons which orbited other planets. The governments of these planets and moons formed an organisation called the United Planets. The organisation's headquarters was on Luna.

Project Spaceguard protected all the inhabited planets and moons in the Solar System. Spaceguard's astronomers watched the sky, night and day, using powerful telescopes. Many of these

14

sky-watchers studied asteroids. By 2130, Spaceguard's computers had tracked and catalogued[19] half a million asteroids. Five of these objects were huge – they were more than 200 kilometres wide. But most of them were quite small pieces of rock which travelled on regular orbits through space. And none of them was going to be a problem to any part of the Solar System.

Then, in 2131, an object was discovered beyond the orbit of the planet Jupiter. When the object was first seen, nobody thought that it was a danger to humans. It was too far away from any planet or moon in the United Planets Organisation. The object was catalogued as 31/439, because it was the 439th object to be discovered that year. But was it an asteroid?

The astronomers realised immediately that the object was bigger than most asteroids. It was at least 40 kilometres wide, and probably bigger than that. And soon the astronomers knew that there was something even more unusual about it – it was not travelling on a regular orbit. This object was coming straight towards the centre of the Solar System!

The astronomers at Project Spaceguard were very excited about this object. They wanted to give it a name. They liked to give a name, not just a catalogue number, for any object in space that was especially interesting. The planets and moons of the Solar System, apart from Earth itself, had names from Ancient Greek and Roman stories. They had been given the names of gods and goddesses in those stories. But they had been named centuries before. The names of Indian gods of the Hindu religion were now being used for newly discovered objects. So this new large object in the sky was named 'Rama'.

The astronomers at Spaceguard were puzzled by Rama. At first they had thought that it was an asteroid. But it was very large and it was not travelling on a regular orbit. And there was another way in which it did not behave like an asteroid. Asteroids have irregular shapes, and they spin round and round as they travel. An asteroid in the Solar System reflects light from the Sun. An astronomer, watching it with a telescope, will see this light getting stronger and weaker as the rock spins through space. These changes are caused by the irregular shape of the asteroid. The light which Rama reflected did not change in strength, so the scientists thought that Rama could not be spinning as it travelled through space.

Then one astronomer – a man called William Stenton – made the discovery which led to the truth about Rama. Rama was spinning, but it was spinning at an amazing speed. Earth makes one turn on its axis in 24 hours. A large asteroid usually takes several hours to rotate. But Rama was taking only four minutes to make one complete turn.

'This is impossible!' Dr Stenton told himself when he first measured Rama's speed of rotation. 'An object of Rama's size, spinning at that speed, should have broken up long ago.'

Stenton checked his mathematical calculations again and again, but he had not made a mistake. And he could think of only one explanation. Perhaps Rama was not an asteroid, but a collapsed star[20] – a dead sun. If it was a collapsed star, Rama had to be very, very heavy and it would be a terrible danger to Earth and to the whole Solar System. Stenton told Spaceguard Headquarters about his calculations at once.

The leaders of the United Planets met on Luna to discuss the problem. Was Rama a danger to their worlds? They could not agree about this. But, as usual, their arguments were really about money, not about possible danger. What could be done to find out more about Rama? A space-probe[21] could be sent to take photos of the strange object, but that would be very expensive. Was Rama so dangerous that the United Planets had to spend a huge amount of money on a space-probe? The leaders argued for a long time, but in the end the answer was yes. They all agreed that humans had to find out more about this strange visitor to the Solar System.

Three months later, a space-probe was flying towards Rama to discover the truth about it. As it got close to the object, small flying cameras were sent out from the probe. The cameras flew past Rama and took photos of it from many different positions. The pictures were transmitted[22] to Spaceguard's scientists. Soon, they were watching the pictures on their TV screens.

The pictures told the scientists two things. Rama was an enormous object, and it was not an asteroid. In fact, it was not a natural object – it had been designed and built by something, or someone!

Rama was a huge cylinder[23], about 50 kilometres long. Its ends were flat, and they were about 20 kilometres in diameter. The surface of the cylinder was a dark grey colour. There was one darker area on the surface, about one kilometre long. Somewhere, during Rama's journey through space, it had been hit by another object. But the cylinder had not been damaged when this happened. That told the scientists that it was made from something very strong.

Soon, the scientists were able to find out the exact weight of the cylinder. And this told them something else. Rama was not solid – it was hollow. So what was inside it? Was the huge, hollow cylinder a spaceship of some kind? Were humans going to receive their first visitors from a world beyond the Solar System?

A group of scientists and politicians – the Rama Committee – was asked to find answers to these questions. They studied the photos from the probe's cameras, and other information from the astronomers. Every member of the Committee had a different idea about Rama. However, they all agreed that the cylinder had to be studied more closely, before it was too late. A fast spaceship must immediately be sent on a mission to meet Rama – to rendezvous with it.

2

Rendezvous With Rama

*E*ndeavour was the fastest spaceship in the Solar System. William Tsien Norton, her commander, was a clever and experienced officer. The Rama Committee decided that Commander Norton was the best person to find out more about Rama.

Endeavour, which was quite a small spaceship, took extra fuel and supplies, and set off for its rendezvous with Rama. It was a long journey and Rama was within the orbit of Venus when *Endeavour* caught up with[24] it. Commander Norton knew that he had only three weeks to explore Rama. After that, the huge cylinder would be too near the Sun and *Endeavour* would not be able to stay with it.

On Earth, on Luna, and on the other inhabited planets and moons, men and women watched their TV screens and waited. Norton was keeping his ship positioned 1000 metres in front of the circular north end of Rama as the cylinder travelled through space. Norton had chosen to land at Rama's north end because that end was in the full light of the Sun.

The Commander had often landed spaceships on moons and planets, of course, but those were natural objects. Rama was not natural. It had been made by someone – or something.

The enormous cylinder was a spaceship of some kind. But if Rama was a spaceship, it was a very, very big one. To Norton and his crew, the cylinder seemed to fill the whole sky.

Rama was spinning on its long axis. Norton had to land his 5000-tonne spaceship safely on the end of the spinning cylinder. He did not hurry. He thought carefully about the difficulties of the landing. The end of the cylinder was like a spinning disc. Norton needed to land close to the centre of the disc. If he tried to land *Endeavour* anywhere else, the speed of Rama's rotation would throw the ship off immediately. But if he landed

*Rama was not natural. It had been made by someone
– or something.*

at the centre, where the speed of rotation was slower, there would be time to fasten the ship to the surface of Rama.

At the centre of the north end of the huge cylinder, there was a circular groove. The groove was about 100 metres in diameter. Norton guessed that this circle was the door of some kind of airlock[25], which would allow smaller spaceships to leave and enter Rama. Norton was worried about landing *Endeavour* here because his ship would be damaged if something inside Rama tried to use this airlock. But if he didn't land close to the axis of the cylinder, he would not be able to land at all.

Commander Norton allowed *Endeavour* to get closer to the surface of the spinning disc. When he looked more carefully at the circular groove, he saw something interesting. Close to its edge, there were three upright cylinders – cylinders which were standing on their ends. Each cylinder was about ten metres in diameter. They were 120 degrees apart.

Norton saw that there was an area between these cylinders big enough to land *Endeavour*. And if Rama's rotation started to move *Endeavour* out towards the edge of the disc, the ship would move against two of these cylinders, and they would hold it. Then the crew could fasten the ship to Rama's surface.

Norton gave instructions to his crew.

Fifteen minutes later, Commander Norton sent a short radio message to the Rama Committee.

'*Endeavour* has landed,' he told them.

The surface of Rama was a completely silent place. Norton had expected to hear the deep sound of motors, or the hum of a radio signal. But his ship's microphones[26] were hearing nothing at all.

The crew of *Endeavour* looked down from their ship at the top of the huge cylinder. There was no movement anywhere. Nothing came out of an airlock to meet them. Was Rama a dead world? Or was it just sleeping? Norton didn't know the answer to this question. Somehow, he had to get inside this strange, vast object. Then he might have an answer.

However, before he could do anything else, he had to fasten his spaceship to the surface of Rama. He did this with strong cables[27]. Then he made his preparations for the first EVA[28] very carefully. On any mission, the first expedition[29] away from a spaceship was always the most important. The Commander didn't want anything to go wrong.

Norton decided to take Lieutenant-Commander Karl Mercer, with him. Mercer was Norton's second-in-command. Two other crewmembers put on their spacesuits too. They would stay on *Endeavour*, but they would be ready to help if they were needed.

Norton used the jets on his spacesuit to move carefully to the nearest of the three upright cylinders. He moved slowly around it, studying it very carefully.

At first, the wall of this cylinder looked completely smooth. But then Norton stopped moving. He had seen something very strange.

'Mercer, come and look at this,' he said into the microphone in his helmet.

Norton had seen six straight grooves in the wall of the cylinder. The deep grooves radiated from a central 'hub', and there was a metal bar within each groove. This made the bars look like the spokes of a wheel.

Norton saw that there was space for him to put his hands into the grooves and hold two of these spokes.

'That's interesting,' Karl Mercer said. 'Do the creatures who live here have hands like ours? Or do the Ramans have curved claws, like animals?'

Norton smiled and gently pulled at two of the spokes. They moved easily out of their grooves, and away from the wall of the upright cylinder. In a moment, Norton was holding a wheel! He waited for a few seconds, but no alarms[30] sounded inside Rama.

Everything was still quiet.

'What do we do now?' Mercer asked. 'Are you going to turn this wheel? It probably opens an airlock of some kind.'

'Karl, what do you think about this?' Norton replied. 'Do you think that this is safe?'

'How can I know?' Mercer said. 'But now that we're here, we must do everything that we can to get inside this strange spaceship.'

Norton tried to turn the wheel to the right, but it wouldn't move. Then Mercer helped him to try again, but there was still no movement.

'Try turning it the other way,' Mercer suggested.

When Norton tried to turn the wheel in the opposite direction, it moved easily. And half a metre away from the wheel, a section of the curved wall of the upright cylinder began to move. It moved outwards, to make an opening like a doorway. Air and dust came from the opening. The men could feel the air on their spacesuits. And the tiny pieces of dust shone in the strong light of the Sun.

'Well, this *is* an airlock,' Mercer said. 'The other two cylinders are probably airlocks too. But this is our way into Rama.'

Norton agreed. But he was a very careful man. Good spaceship commanders never take risks[31]. Before his crew explored any further, Norton wanted to return to *Endeavour* and send another report to the Rama Committee.

The two men closed the airlock and returned to their ship. Commander Norton sent his report and waited for a reply.

As usual, the scientists of the Rama Committee argued amongst themselves. But in the end, their decision was clear. The exploration of Rama had to continue.

———

Two days later, the members of the Committee received a longer report.

'The other two cylinders are probably airlocks too. But this is
our way into Rama.'

From: Commander W.T. Norton
To: Rama Committee, Luna

....

Everything is OK here. We passed safely through the first set of air-locks. There were three of them – one after another – below the upright cylinder which we entered. We guess that there are similar sets of airlocks below the other two upright cylinders. This number – three – seems important to the Ramans!

We checked everything as we moved forward, and we sent mobile cameras[32] ahead of us. We shut the first airlock before entering the second, and we shut the second before we went through the third. We cannot take any risks here.

A straight corridor led onwards from the third airlock. This corridor was nearly half a kilometre long. It was completely dark in there. We had to use our flashlights when we explored the corridor.

At the end of this corridor, we found another set of three airlocks. Beyond those, is the interior of Rama. We opened the last door, but we went no further. We need your permission to continue exploring. We have returned to our ship to wait for your answer.

W.T. Norton (Commander, *Endeavour*)

As he waited for an answer from the Rama Committee, Norton remembered an old story from Earth history. At the beginning of the twentieth century, an archeologist called Howard Carter had found the tomb of Tutankhamen, a king of Ancient Egypt. Inside the tomb was a room full of treasure – gold, jewels and all kinds of wonderful things.

'Perhaps Rama is also a tomb. And perhaps it is full of wonderful things,' Norton thought. 'Well, we shall soon know.'

3

Into the Darkness

The Rama Committee gave Commander Norton permission to continue the exploration of Rama. Norton had to report back to the Committee often, but he was now in full control of the mission. He would make decisions about where the members of his crew would go and how they would work.

First he made a decision about how he and his crew would divide up their time. The members of the crew came from several different parts of the Solar System – Earth, Mars and Luna. But when they were in space, they used a twenty-four hour clock, like the one used on Earth. So although it seemed to be completely dark inside Rama, Norton decided that the crew would divide their time into 'days' and 'nights'. Most of them would work during the days and sleep during the nights.

Once again, William Norton and Karl Mercer moved slowly along the corridor which they had already visited. The jets on their spacesuits were pushing them forward. The two men were carrying big flashlights.

They reached the far end of the corridor and closed the first two airlocks behind them. And this time, Norton went through the third airlock too. He attached one end of a safety line[33] to the door and the other end to his spacesuit. Then he moved forward into the interior of Rama. Like the corridor, the interior was completely dark.

As Norton had expected, there was no gravity beyond the airlock. As he drifted forward into the darkness, he suddenly felt a little afraid. He had walked in space many times. But this was different. He took a deep breath and shone his flashlight around him.

Norton was drifting in a place that was like a large bowl with smooth walls. Within this bowl, he could see two other doors and he guessed that they led to two other sets of airlocks.

'Yes, there are always three of everything,' he told himself. 'The number must be important to the Ramans.'

As Norton looked around, he understood something. The bowl he was in was at the bottom of a much larger bowl or hemisphere, whose sides curved up into the darkness above his head. In the beam of his flashlight, he could see stairways ascending the walls of this hemisphere. But he could not see how far up they went.

'I can't see far enough with the flashlight. I'm going to send up a flare[34],' Norton reported to Mercer, over his radio. 'There will be a delay of two minutes, then the flare will light up. By then, I'll have my camera ready.'

Norton threw the flare straight up into the huge bowl and waited. Then, as the bright light burned, the Commander took his first photos of the strange, silent world of Rama.

Norton's first view of Rama's interior lasted for only two minutes, but he tried to keep the picture in his mind. He was at one end of the huge hollow cylinder. He could just see the curved wall of the cylinder all around him. He already knew that the outside of Rama was about 20 kilometres in diameter. The interior wall that he could see was about nine kilometres away from him in every direction. The cylinder was about 50 kilometres long and Norton couldn't see right to the other end of it – the light from his flare could not reach the far end. In that direction – and for the moment Norton thought of that direction as 'up' – the interior of Rama faded into the darkness.

Norton had no time to understand the details of this new world. He saw only light and shadow, and a strange band of darkness. About 15 kilometres from the north end, this band of darkness seemed to extend[35] right around the cylinder wall.

The huge cylinder was spinning on its axis as it moved through space. This rotation was creating a special kind of gravity inside Rama. Where he was drifting, close to the axis,

*...as the bright light burned, he took his first photos of the
strange, silent world of Rama.*

Norton felt completely weightless. But he knew that if he stood on the inside of the cylinder wall, he would feel the effect of Rama's gravity. There, his body would have weight and he would not drift above the ground. He would be able to walk on the wall, with his head towards the cylinder's axis.

Norton knew something else too. Although he felt that he was looking up into Rama, he was also looking down into it. He was weightless where he was, so there was no difference between 'up' and 'down'. But he was at the north end of the cylinder. He thought of north as the top, and he thought of south as the bottom. So he was now at the cylinder's highest point, not at its lowest point. He had to get used to this idea.

After the light from the flare had faded, Norton thought about these things. He was in darkness again. But he had had his first view of Rama's interior. He would remember that for the rest of his life!

———

Two days later, on Luna, the members of the Rama Committee were holding a conference. They were studying the maps and photos which Norton had sent to them across space.

Professor Olaf Davidson looked up from his map and spoke.

'Let's hear Norton's last audio report again,' the famous astronomer said. 'We must try to understand everything that he saw. The details of the inside of this cylinder are very puzzling.'

Norton's audio report was played back[36] to the Committee. The Commander's voice sounded very clear.

'We've now sent up some more long-delay flares and we've photographed the whole length of the cylinder by their light,' the Commander's voice told them. 'You all have copies of those photos and the maps that we've made. The photos and maps show the main details of the interior. We've given names to all these things, to make it easier for you to understand our reports.

'The inside of the cylinder is about 48 kilometres long. Its diameter is more than 18 kilometres. The two ends are concave inside – like the insides of huge bowls. Our first camp is near the airlocks at the north end. We call this end of Rama the Northern Hemisphere. We call the small circular bowl around the airlocks the Hub, because it's like the centre of a wheel. There are three ladders leading away from the Hub. The ladders are 120 degrees apart. Each ladder is about one kilometre long, and they lead from the Hub to a circular terrace[37]. We call this the Inner Terrace. We've named the three ladders Alpha, Beta and Gamma.

'From the Inner Terrace, three very long stairways lead on from the ladders, out towards the cylinder wall. The three stairways are like the spokes of a wheel. The stairways – Alpha, Beta and Gamma Stairways – are divided into sections by other circular terraces. These terraces are concentric[38] with the Inner Terrace. And each stairway has about 30,000 big steps.

'The other end of the cylinder – we call it the Southern Hemisphere – is completely different,' Norton's voice continued. 'It has no stairways and no central hub. But a huge spike[39] extends along the axis from its centre point. We call this central point the South Pole. The spike seems to be several kilometres long. And there are six more spikes, smaller ones, around the large one. We don't understand what these spikes are used for.

'We have named the area between the two Hemispheres, the Central Plain. It isn't really a plain, of course, because it isn't flat. It's a curved surface – it's the interior wall of Rama. But when we start to walk along the Plain, it will look flat, because the diameter of the cylinder is so vast. We'll be like tiny ants crawling inside a bottle!

'About halfway along the Central Plain there is an area which looks darker than the rest. It seems to be a band about ten kilometres wide. It extends right around the cylinder wall, like a ring. We think that the band might be made of ice, so we have called it the Cylindrical Sea. In this sea there is a large island, with tall shapes on it. The shapes look like the buildings that people used to call skyscrapers. So we've named the island, New York. We don't think that the place is really a city. Perhaps it's a factory[40].

'But there are other places on the Central Plain that may be cities. We've named them London, Paris, Rome, Moscow, Beijing, Tokyo, etc. You can see these on the map that we have sent. The cities seem to be joined by roads, and perhaps by railways too.

'There is so much to see in this huge, silent, frozen place. There's so much to think about too. There are thousands of square kilometres[41] to explore. We could spend years trying to understand Rama, and we have only a few weeks here. We know that we must leave before the Sun makes Rama too hot for us. But we are very puzzled. What is this place? Who planned it and who made it? What a strange place Rama is!'

The members of the Rama Committee sat in silence for a few minutes after the report ended. Then Dr Carlisle Perera, a well-known biologist, began to speak.

'Well, I think that I can answer some of Commander Norton's questions,' he said. 'I've always believed that there is life in the Universe outside the Solar System. And I've always believed that there are living beings in other parts of our Galaxy. Rama proves this. That cylinder is a huge spaceship and it wasn't made anywhere in the Solar System – we know that. But now it's a ship without any life. It's cold, dark and empty.'

'So what went wrong?' someone asked.

'We shall probably never know the answer to that,' Dr Perera replied. 'Rama has been travelling through space for at least 200,000 years. We know that, because we can track Rama's path back through space, and we know its speed. We know that the last time it was close to a star was about 200,000 years ago. Perhaps that star was the Ramans' sun. Perhaps Rama was made on a planet which orbited that star. Or perhaps Rama came from somewhere far beyond that star. Perhaps its journey started much more than 200,000 years ago. Perhaps Rama has been travelling for a million years!

'The spaceship that we call Rama is a closed world,' Perera continued. 'Worlds like that can't last for ever. The Ramans who started the journey must have died long ago. And although other Ramans were probably born on the ship, something must have happened which killed them. The Ramans needed something like air to breathe. We know that because Norton has found airlocks leading into Rama. Perhaps all the air inside the cylinder was used up[42].

'Or perhaps there was an illness which killed everything within the closed world. Perhaps the Ramans didn't plan such a long trip. Perhaps the ship travelled on a wrong course. As I said, we shall probably never know the truth.

'But one thing is certain now – we are not alone in the Universe. There are other living beings out there among the stars. At last, we have a chance to learn something about them. Commander Norton and his crew must explore the whole of Rama, before it's too late!'

4

Up or Down?

Soon, everything was ready for a short expedition into the interior of Rama. Norton had wanted to lead the expedition himself, but he decided that he should stay at the Hub this time. Then if something went wrong, he could lead the rest of his crew to safety.

Norton chose three men to go into the interior of Rama. Karl Mercer was the leader of the team. Two other experienced crewmembers – Lieutenant Joe Calvert and Technical-Sergeant

Willard Myron – would go with him. Three was the right number of people for an exploring team. If one man was killed, the other two could help each other escape from danger. But was there danger inside Rama? The team could soon find out!

Mercer and his team were going to climb on Alpha Ladder, then move along the Alpha Stairway which continued from it. They were well equipped. They were each carrying equipment which would weigh about 100 kilos on Earth. They had no problem carrying this weight near the Hub, because there was zero gravity at Rama's axis. As they moved away from the axis, the equipment would feel heavier and heavier. But Norton didn't want the team to go all the way to the Central Plain on this first journey.

Norton went with the three explorers to the beginning of Alpha Ladder. They all stood for a minute at the edge of the Hub, looking along the ladder.

'Are we climbing *down*, or are we climbing *up*?' Mercer asked himself. 'Are we *descending* a cliff or are we *ascending* a wall?'

Mercer decided to go head-first on the ladder. For the first few hundred metres, in the zero-gravity area, he would feel that he was ascending. He would be pulling himself along the ladder with his hands and trying to keep his feet on the rungs[43] too. But after a few hundred metres he would begin to feel the effect of the gravity. Then he would think that he was descending. His weight would pull him towards the cylinder wall.

The first 200 metres of the climb was easy. But soon, the explorers could feel the gravity which was beginning to pull them forwards. At the 500th rung of the ladder, Mercer stopped and used the radio in his helmet to talk to the others.

'Are there any problems?' he asked them.

'Everything is OK,' Myron replied. 'But you must both hold onto the ladder very tightly. The gravity is pulling us forward strongly now. And now the rotation of the cylinder on its axis will start to push us to the right. It could push us off the ladder.'

'Yes, it's time to turn around,' Mercer said. 'We need to continue feet-first!'

Mercer and the others turned round carefully, holding on tightly to the ladder. Now they were looking back towards the Hub. Far above them, Commander Norton was standing, watching them. Mercer waved his arm at Norton, then he went slowly backwards down the ladder, rung-by-rung.

After a few minutes, Mercer, Calvert, then Myron had reached the end of the ladder. They were all standing on the terrace which separated the end of Alpha Ladder from the beginning of Alpha Stairway. This terrace – which they had named Level One – was a narrow, flat ledge. The explorers looked at the stairway which went on down into the darkness. The stairway had a handrail[44].

'We'll have to hold on tightly to the handrail,' Mercer said. 'There still isn't much gravity here. If we go too fast on the stairway, the spin of the cylinder will throw us off the stairs. It will throw us seven kilometres down to the wall. We must be very careful!'

The three men began to walk down the stairs. It was difficult for them because the steps were very large.

'I think that these steps were made for beings with longer legs than ours,' Calvert said. 'Let's slide down the handrail!'

'OK, let's do it!' Mercer answered with a laugh.

The three men sat on the handrail, with one leg on either side. Carefully, they started to slide down the rail. In two minutes, they had moved a kilometre nearer to the Plain and they had reached the next flat, circular terrace. This was Level Two. They rested here, at the top of the next part of the stairway. It was a good time to make a report to Commander Norton.

'Commander, we are all OK,' Mercer reported. 'We are resting at Level Two. The temperature hasn't changed – it's below the freezing point[45] of water. But my instruments tell me that there is air with plenty of oxygen in it at this level. I think that

After a few minutes, Mercer, Calvert, then Myron had reached the end of the ladder.

we can breathe it. I'm going to try doing that.'

Mercer carefully opened the helmet of his spacesuit. He took one breath, then another. The air inside Rama was dry and it didn't smell fresh, but it didn't harm him. That told Mercer something which was good to know. When they went down to the Central Plain, *Endeavour*'s explorers would not need their breathing equipment after Level Two.

But Mercer decided that the next part of the exploration would have to wait.

'The air here is OK,' he told Norton. 'But we're coming back now. We can go all the way down next time.'

'Right,' said Norton. 'Start on your return journey when you're ready. Don't hurry. The climb will make you tired.'

Now Mercer, Calvert and Myron had to climb up the stairs. That was much more difficult than sliding down the rail. The first 200 steps on the stairway were quite easy for the explorers. Then they began to feel tired. It took them about ten minutes to reach Level One. They stopped there to rest, and then they went on to the Inner Terrace and the ladder.

The three men moved slowly on Alpha Ladder, but at last they reached the Hub. This first journey into Rama's interior had taken about an hour, but the explorers had travelled only about a quarter of the distance down to the Central Plain.

———

The *Endeavour*'s doctor gave the three explorers a careful medical check when they returned to the ship.

'Mercer and Calvert are fine,' Surgeon-Commander Laura Ernst told Norton. 'Myron is very tired. He isn't very fit. He needs to rest. He mustn't go into Rama again for a day or two.

'But there won't be too many problems for the explorers,' Dr Ernst went on. 'Beyond Level Two, they won't have to carry breathing equipment – they'll only have to carry food and water. They will need their thermo-suits[46] though, because the air is so cold.'

35

'OK,' said Norton. 'Can the next expedition go right down to the Central Plain? What do you think about that?'

'Well, going down will be easy, if they slide down the handrails,' Laura Ernst replied. 'Climbing back up will be slow and tiring. But we don't have much time here, so I think that the next team should go all the way to the Plain!'

'Good, that's what I think too,' Norton said. 'This time, I'll lead the team myself. I'll take Joe. I'll also take Boris Rodrigo. He's strong and very fit. He's always calm too. He will be a great help to me.' The Commander turned to Mercer. 'I'll leave you in charge[47] at the Hub, Karl. Make a camp there. We'll call the camp Hub Control. We'll need a strong searchlight there to show us our way on the Central Plain. And there must be a telescope at Hub Control too. Then you can warn us if you see any Ramans!'

It was very cold inside Rama – very cold and very, very quiet. Norton, Rodrigo and Calvert left their breathing equipment on the ledge at Level Two. Then they went on.

At Level Five, the effect of gravity was much stronger. Here, it was about half of Earth's gravity, so they walked down the stairs. The journey so far had been quite easy. But the three men knew that the return journey would take all their strength.

As the explorers got closer to the wall of the cylinder – the beginning of the Central Plain – the steps of the stairway became lower. It was much easier to walk down them. The last part of the journey to the Plain was the most comfortable part.

At the end of the stairway, the three men stood for a few minutes. They looked towards Hub Control, more than eight kilometres above their heads. The beam of the searchlight was shining down and they knew that Mercer was watching them through the telescope. Norton waved his arm towards Karl Mercer, then spoke to him on his radio.

'This is Norton,' he said. 'It's very cold down here on the

Plain. It's still below freezing point. And it's very, very quiet. But there's something strange about this place. It doesn't look as if anything or anybody has ever been here before. Everything here looks new and unused.'

'Does the place where you are now tell you anything new about the Ramans?' Mercer asked. 'What were they like – what do you think?'

'Well, they breathed oxygen, like us,' Norton replied. 'Perhaps they looked like us too. They must have had things like hands and legs because they made these ladders and stairs. But we think that the Ramans were taller than humans. The distance between the rungs of the ladders and the height of the steps of the stairways makes us think that. Perhaps we'll find out more as we go on.

'The nearest things that are like buildings are about eight kilometres from here,' Norton continued. 'That's the place that we named Paris. I'd like to go on and look at Paris during this expedition. What does Doctor Ernst think about that?'

Laura Ernst studied the information that the instruments in the men's thermo-suits were sending back to her. She was able to give the explorers medical checks in this way.

'You're all fine,' she told Norton after a few minutes. 'I think that you should go on. And good luck to you all!'

The three men started to walk along the Central Plain, towards the other end of Rama. The powerful beam of the searchlight at Hub Control made a path through the darkness in front of them and around them. To the right and left of the explorers, the floor of the cylinder curved upwards. The curve was not steep because Rama's diameter was so huge. But the surface beneath their feet went on curving at either side of them, until it became the 'sky' above their heads.

The explorers were going to visit the group of buildings that they had called Paris. But there was something else that they wanted to investigate before they got to Paris. Their photos, taken by the light of the flares, had shown some large grooves in the wall of the cylinder. There were six of these strange grooves, which followed the direction of Rama's axis. Three of them were on the north side of the Cylindrical Sea. They were 120 degrees apart, on the curve of Rama's wall. The grooves extended as far as the north 'cliff' at the Sea's edge. The other three grooves began opposite the first set, at the high southern cliff of the Sea. Each of the grooves was about ten kilometres long.

When he'd made his map, Norton had given a name to the groove closest to where they were now. He'd named it the Straight Valley. It was about one kilometre from them now, and they were walking towards it.

About ten minutes later, Norton and his team were looking down into Straight Valley. It was about 40 metres deep and 100 metres wide. Its sloping[48] sides, which were the same grey colour as Rama's walls, were completely smooth. But the bottom of the valley was white. It looked smooth too.

'Is that ice at the bottom of the valley?' Calvert asked.

'I don't know,' Norton replied. 'I'll go down there. I don't see any steps, so you'll have to let me down on a safety line.'

Norton was soon at the bottom of the valley. He touched the white surface carefully. It was more like glass than ice – it was cold but it wasn't slippery. But it wasn't transparent – he couldn't see through it.

38

Norton took a small hammer[49] from a pocket in his thermo-suit and he hit the white surface with it. Nothing happened. He hit it again, harder this time. But suddenly he had a strange thought.

'This is wrong!' he thought. 'I mustn't damage this beautiful, smooth, flat surface. I don't want to. I mustn't damage anything in this clean, empty world. Rama must not be harmed.'

Norton looked slowly around him. He still thought that everything inside Rama looked new and unused. But that was impossible!

'Everything here must be hundreds of thousands of years old,' he told himself. 'I can't understand this!'

'Pull me up,' he called to Calvert and Rodrigo. 'There's nothing important down here. We'll go on to Paris now.'

———

If Paris was a city, it was a strange one. It was a disappointing place for the men from *Endeavour*.

There were several hundred 'buildings', standing on wide, empty streets. All the buildings were the same – each one had a rectangular shape and was 35 metres high. The buildings seemed to grow out of the Plain, and they were made of the same material as the Plain. There were no joints between the buildings and the streets. The strangest thing of all was that these buildings had no doors or windows. The explorers couldn't find out whether the buildings were hollow.

'No one lives here, and no one has ever lived here,' Norton said. 'These buildings aren't houses. They can't be houses – there is no way into them, or out of them.'

'But look at this groove,' Joe Calvert said. He pointed at the ground by his feet. There was a narrow groove in the street, about five centimetres wide. 'There are grooves like this one along every street. And every groove stops at the wall of one of the buildings.'

'Perhaps the grooves are part of a transport system,' Rodrigo said. 'Perhaps these buildings are used to store supplies.'

'But what could the Ramans store here?' Norton asked. 'And how do they get to their stores? There's no way that we can get inside these buildings without explosives or powerful laser beams[50]. We'll have to photograph all this and send the photos back to the Committee. Perhaps the members of the Committee will know the answers to our questions!'

5

Storm Warning

Some time later, the members of the Rama Committee were studying the latest photos which Norton had sent them. The photos of Paris interested them the most.

'If Paris is a city, it's a very strange one – Commander Norton is right about that,' said Dr Thelma Price. Doctor Price was an archeologist. 'Norton thinks that the buildings could be used for storing things,' she went on. 'And I agree with him. The entrances to the buildings may be under the surface of the ground. But Norton couldn't get into the buildings and he doesn't want to use explosives or lasers. He doesn't want to be the first man to destroy any part of Rama. I can understand his feelings.'

'I have a different idea,' said Dennis Solomons, who was a historian. 'These buildings might be the Ramans' museums. The ancient objects inside them might have been sealed[51] in there to protect them from the air. We've often done that on Earth.'

'Well, that might be true,' said Dr Perera. 'But I have something more important to tell this Committee. Commander Norton and his crew may be in great danger! Let me explain.

'The Commander has told us that the interior of Rama is very cold at the moment. The temperature is below freezing point. But Rama is getting nearer and nearer to the Sun. The outside temperature of the cylinder must now be about 500 degrees. The wall of Rama is very thick – we know that. But soon, the Sun's heat will have travelled through the wall to the interior. The thinnest part of the wall is probably the part at the bottom of the Cylindrical Sea. The heat will get through the wall there first. If the Cylindrical Sea is made of ice, it will start to melt. And the air temperature inside the cylinder will start to rise. That will lead to the main problem.'

'And what is that?' Dr Bose, the elderly Ambassador for Mars asked. 'Please tell us.'

'I can give you the answer in one word – hurricanes[52],' Dr Perera replied. 'The air nearest the wall inside Rama is getting hotter as Rama gets closer to the Sun. That air has been spinning at more than 800 kilometres an hour. Soon, the hot air will expand and it will rise quickly towards the cylinder's central axis. At the axis, the air will slow down. The result will be winds inside Rama. There will be strong winds and dreadful storms. That is what will put Commander Norton and the crew of *Endeavour* in terrible danger. We must send them a warning. They must get out of Rama – they must get out now!'

———

Commander Norton had no idea that he was in danger. There were now twenty men and women from *Endeavour*'s crew working inside Rama. Six of them were exploring the Central Plain. They explored in two teams of three people. The others were busy bringing food, water and equipment down Alpha Stairway to the camp on the Plain at the end of it. This was now named Alpha Camp.

One of the teams on the Plain was led by Dr Laura Ernst. The other two members of her team were Boris Rodrigo and Sergeant Pieter Rousseau. Rousseau had a small telescope which he used often as the team moved along the Plain. This team's aim was to reach the Cylindrical Sea and find out more about it.

These three experienced crewmembers had walked nearly 15 kilometres through the silent darkness of Rama. Their path was lit by the beam of the powerful searchlight at Hub Control. They were unable to see anything beyond the circle of light which they were walking in. They reported to Hub Control after every kilometre that they walked.

'The Cylindrical Sea is only about 100 metres from where you are now,' Hub Control told them at last. 'You must slow down a little. You mustn't fall into it!'

A few moments later, the three explorers had reached the cliff and they were looking down at the Sea. But was it a sea? And was it made of ice? Nothing about Rama was certain.

The explorers were standing at the top of a low cliff and the surface of the Cylindrical Sea was only about 50 metres below them. But they knew from their photos that the cliff on the other side of the Sea – the southern side – was 500 metres high. What was the reason for this? Could they find out?

They felt nervous and excited. As they looked ahead, the surface of the Sea seemed flat. But to the left and the right, the surface of the Sea curved upwards. It was a frightening sight.

Doctor Ernst called Hub Control.

'Please point the searchlight beam at New York,' she said.

The beam shone out across the Sea to the island. The tall shapes of New York appeared out of the darkness and the three explorers stared at them in silence.

Ernst, Rodrigo and Rousseau could see several kinds of building in the beam of the searchlight. There were tall towers and there were domes[53]. There were spheres too, and these were joined by large tubes or pipes. In some places, the searchlight's beam was reflected back from a smooth surface. For a moment, the explorers thought that these reflections might be signals. They looked for some movement on the island. They hoped

The tall shapes of New York appeared out of the darkness …

that somebody or something was trying to communicate with them. But nothing was moving in New York.

The explorers began to walk slowly along the cliff, looking for a way down it. At last they found one – a narrow stairway.

Laura Ernst went down carefully. At the bottom of the stairway, she put one foot on the surface of the Sea. It still looked like ice, and it felt slippery. Yes, it was ice.

Laura took a few steps forward, then she took a hammer and a small glass bottle from a pocket in her thermo-suit. She cracked the surface of the ice with the hammer and put some small pieces of it into the bottle. Immediately, the pieces of ice began to melt into a liquid. The liquid was not clear, and it had a bad smell.

'It's water!' Laura called to the others. 'The Cylindrical Sea is made of water. But I wouldn't like to drink it. I'm coming up now.'

Back at the top of the cliff, the doctor looked at the bottle again. 'It only seems to be dirty water,' she said. 'But it might tell us a lot about Rama. Let's get back to Alpha Camp now.'

As the team moved back towards the north, Laura Ernst had a surprise. Suddenly, she felt a gentle wind on her face. But it only lasted for a moment, and she didn't say anything about it to the others.

––––––

A few hours later, both the exploring teams were back at Alpha Camp. Laura had studied the water from the Cylindrical Sea and she was reporting to Commander Norton.

'The liquid contains carbon compounds, phosphates and nitrates, as well as metallic salts[54],' she explained. 'All these things are needed for life. But there are no living things in this liquid. And it has never contained life.'

Norton was disappointed to hear Laura's words. He had hoped to find some form of life on Rama.

Norton thought about the information that the expeditions

had collected. Paris, with its strange rectangular buildings, all the same height, was probably used to store things. But it was a place without windows or doors. Nothing had ever lived there. London was silent and empty too. Its wide streets crossed each other at 90 degrees, and there were long high buildings on both sides of the streets. But like the buildings in Paris, London's buildings had no doors or windows. The explorers had been unable to enter any of them. Rama was keeping its secrets!

The Commander had another problem. He had just received a message from the Rama Committee which he didn't understand. The message was a warning about winds blowing at 300 kilometres an hour. Everything inside the huge cylinder was completely calm. However, it was true that the temperature inside Rama was rising. It was now a little above freezing point.

As Norton thought about this, he felt a gentle wind moving his hair.

'Perhaps the scientists are right,' he thought. 'But there's no danger yet. I can get everyone back to safety in two hours. That will be enough.'

He sent a short reply to the Committee.

From: Commander W.T. Norton
To: The Rama Committee, Luna

....

Thank you for your message. Everything is calm here at the present time. We will leave only when I feel that we are in danger.

6

Light!

Later that 'night' – the hours of sleep for most of *Endeavour*'s crew – the men and women at Alpha Camp were woken by terrifying sounds.

First there was a loud cracking sound. This was followed by several crashing sounds, one after the other. Each crash sounded like thousands of windows being broken at the same time.

Norton called Hub Control on his radio. 'What was that?' he asked. 'What's happened? Report, please!'

'The sounds are coming from the Sea,' Hub Control reported. 'We're shining the searchlight at it now.'

Nine kilometres above the camp, the searchlight was switched on. Its beam reached out across the Plain. It showed the crew an amazing sight.

The Cylindrical Sea was moving and changing. Huge pieces of ice were being pushed upwards. They shone in the light for a moment, then fell back into water.

The ice was breaking up. Parts of the Sea were now liquid. It was the ice at the bottom of the Sea – the ice nearest to the cylinder wall – that was turning to water. As it did this, it was contracting. There was suddenly an empty space between the ice at the surface of the sea and the water below it. Then the ice fell into the water, breaking into thousands of pieces.

The dreadful crashing sounds went on and on.

'Soon, all the ice will melt as the temperature of the cylinder wall rises,' Norton thought.

And as he thought this, he felt the wind on his face again. It was a little stronger than before. The wind was a warning. It was time to leave Rama!

———

No one was killed or injured when the ice broke up. But the explorers' ascent of Alpha Stairway was slow and difficult.

Norton was the last of *Endeavour*'s crew to leave Alpha Camp. He was very disappointed. He had found out very little about Rama and he felt that his mission had failed.

Norton and his crew climbed up and up. At the Second Level, they rested for an hour. From here, there wasn't enough oxygen in the air, and they would have to use their breathing equipment again. They put on their helmets and picked up the heavy oxygen bottles.

After another hour, they reached the end of the stairway. Only Alpha Ladder, one kilometre long, was now between the explorers and the Hub. After another short rest, they were ready for the final part of the climb. This last part of the ascent was difficult. The searchlight's beam could not help them here. The explorers were climbing in the dark.

Everyone else was still in front of Commander Norton. He was getting very tired. He counted each rung of the ladder as he climbed.

Then something amazing happened. The huge cylinder was suddenly filled with light! It was as if Rama's long night was over and dawn had come to it at last!

At first, the light was so bright that Norton had to close his eyes for a minute. Then he opened them and turned around on the ladder. Now his back was pressed against the rungs. The sight in front of him was so amazing that his whole body began to shake. He had to hold on tightly to the ladder. He took several deep breaths and spoke into his microphone.

'This is Norton,' he said. 'Is everyone OK?'

The crew answered one after another. Everybody was OK. Then Norton spoke again.

'Close your eyes for a short time, then look back at the Plain,' he told his crew. 'It's an unbelievable sight! When you've looked, close your eyes again and continue climbing. We're almost at zero gravity here, so you won't fall from the ladder now.'

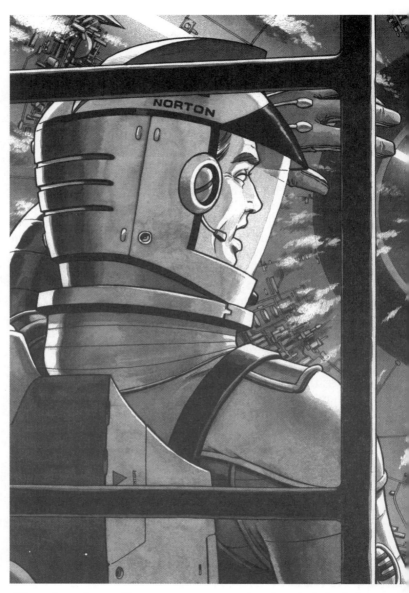

The sight in front of him was so amazing that his whole body began to shake.

Norton had closed his own eyes as he spoke, but now he opened them again. He had to look once more at the interior of this strange world in space. The sight was almost impossible to believe.

All the light was coming from the six deep grooves in the wall of the cylinder – the three grooves on either side of the Cylindrical Sea. The light was a blue colour and it was so strong that it hurt Norton's eyes to look at the grooves.

'Well, now we know what those grooves are for – that's one more thing that we've discovered,' Norton told himself.

But who or what had switched on this bright light? Until a moment ago, Rama had been dark for perhaps a million years. What had ended the long night of Rama? Everyone had thought that there was no life here. Was something being born now? Or was something waking up?

As he asked himself these questions, Norton had felt no fear. He had looked along the whole length of Rama, seeing it all clearly for the first time. As he looked, he had been filled with excitement.

But suddenly the huge size of Rama, which the Commander could now see clearly for the first time, began to have a strange effect on his mind. He asked himself a question.

When he looked along Rama's axis, was he looking up? Or was he looking down? He was an experienced space traveller, but he had been born on Earth. He could never completely forget what his life on Earth had taught him about gravity and geography. If he told himself that he was looking *up*, then the stairways and ladders *descended* from the wall to the Hub. He had to believe that the cities of Rama were fixed to the walls above him. That was possible! But it was harder to believe that the blue water of the Cylindrical Sea was also held half-way up the wall of the cylinder.

And as he thought about this, Norton's understanding of Rama changed. In his mind, the strange world seemed to turn.

Now he thought that he was holding on to a high, curved cliff, and that he was looking *along* the cylinder, not up or down. Now the stairway descended to *the Plain*, eight kilometres below him. This distance was the same as the height of Mount Everest – Earth's highest mountain.

'Looking up from the Plain to the Hub is like looking up at Mount Everest,' Norton thought.

Then a third idea about Rama came into Norton's mind. Now he thought that he was like a fly moving upside-down on a ceiling. And suddenly this thought filled him with terror. The direction *down* was now 50 kilometres to the other end of the cylinder!

Norton tried to stop thinking these frightening thoughts. He checked the time. Only ten minutes had passed since the light had come on inside Rama. But those ten minutes now seemed like many hours. Norton pulled himself slowly up the last hundred metres of the ladder. He stood at the edge of the Hub and looked around again. Would this be his last sight of the strange world of Rama?

Long lines of white mist were coming from the Sea and they were rising towards the axis of the cylinder. At the axis, the lines of mist were moving round and round. They were spinning with the cylinder. Very soon, Rama was going to have its first storm. Doctor Perera had been right – a hurricane was coming. The crew of *Endeavour* was escaping just in time.

'We'll wait in the ship,' Norton told the others. 'Maybe the storm will end soon.'

———

Boris Rodrigo was a religious man. He had his own idea about the reason why Rama had come to the Solar System. Rodrigo visited Commander Norton in his cabin on *Endeavour* and told him about this idea.

'I think that I know the purpose of Rama's journey,' Rodrigo told Norton quietly. 'And now I want to tell you what I believe,

51

Commander Norton.'

'Go on, Boris,' Norton said.

'Rama is a completely lifeless world,' Rodrigo said. 'But it has water, and humans can breathe its air. Everything in Rama is new – I mean that nothing has ever been used, whenever it was made.'

'Yes, we know all this,' Norton said. 'Have you any new ideas about these facts?'

'Yes,' Boris replied. 'Rama has come from deep space. It has come from outside the Solar System. But has it been *sent* into our system? Yes, it has been sent – that cannot have happened by chance.

'I believe that once, long ago, a ship was built on Earth to save men from a terrible disaster,' Boris went on. 'It was built to save good people who believed in God. It was built by a man called Noah – you can read his story in ancient religious books. I think that Rama, too, is a ship which has come to save all good people from a disaster.'

'Well, that's an interesting idea, Boris,' Norton said. 'There are lots of different ideas about Rama, and yours is better than most of them. But there is one problem. In about three weeks' time, Rama will be closer to the Sun than it will ever be again. After that, it will probably fly onwards and leave the Solar System forever.'

'No, I don't agree,' Boris said. 'I believe that Rama will go into orbit around the Sun, and then it will change speed and rendezvous with Earth. I believe that the Earth will be destroyed soon. The people who enter Rama before it leaves the Solar System will be saved when the Earth is destroyed.'

'I understand what you're saying,' Norton replied. 'Perhaps the Rama Committee would like to hear your idea. I'll include your thoughts with my next report. This may be important. Thank you, Boris.'

Norton thought for a moment, then he spoke again.

'How has Rama travelled to the Solar System, Boris?' he asked. 'Have you any ideas about that? We haven't seen or heard anything in Rama which could explain how it travels. What is powering it? What kind of motors does it have?'

Boris Rodrigo shook his head.

'I'm sorry, Commander. I don't know the answers,' he said.

7

The Fears of the Hermians

The next meeting of the Rama Committee was not an easy one. Doctor Perera had told the other members that there would be a storm inside Rama. That had now happened and Perera was pleased to hear about it. But the Hermian Ambassador – the Ambassador for Mercury – wasn't pleased at all when he heard the rest of the news from Rama.

'Commander Norton and his crew must return to the interior of Rama at once,' the Ambassador said. 'They must find out more about Rama – much more. Somebody or something is controlling that cylinder. It is obvious that Rama has a purpose. It has a mission to complete. That mission may be a war – a war against the United Planets. We must get ready to protect ourselves. And we can't do that unless we know more facts about Rama.'

'This talk about war is nonsense!' said another member of the Committee. 'The Ramans are very intelligent beings. They know much more than we do. They must know that wars solve no problems.'

'Perhaps you are right about that,' the Hermian Ambassador replied. 'But perhaps you are wrong! We must all be prepared. The whole of our Solar System may be in great danger. And we

53

Hermians – the people of Mercury – may be in greater danger than anyone else.'

'Why do you say that?' asked Dr Perera.

'Please remember that Mercury is the nearest planet to the Sun,' the Ambassador replied. 'Rama is now travelling inside the orbit of Mercury. What is the next part of the Ramans' plan? Will Rama fly past the Sun, then on, out into space? Or will it change its course?

'If Rama changes its course, it will probably do this when it's about 25 million kilometres from the Sun,' the Ambassador went on. 'Mercury is nearly twice that distance from the Sun, at the closest point of its orbit. Please think about that.'

The members of the Committee were silent. Everybody was thinking about Mercury and the people who lived there. Hermians had always been difficult people, probably because their lives were difficult.

Mercury is a very, very hot world. Its rivers are full of liquid metal, not of water. To protect themselves, the humans on Mercury had always had to live in an artificial environment[55]. Because their lives were so difficult, the Hermians had become tough and clever. They were admired by the inhabitants of the other planets, but they were not really liked. However, Mercury had huge resources[56] of metal and huge resources of energy. These were important to the people of the other planets. The other people of the Solar System had to stay friends with the Hermians.

'If Rama orbits the Sun at a distance of 25 million kilometres, it will change our lives on Mercury,' the Ambassador continued, after a moment. 'Rama will be able to control the resources and the energy of our planet. And very soon the whole Solar System will be under the control of the Ramans, whoever they are!'

'I understand your fears, Ambassador,' the Chairman said at last. 'Have you any suggestions?'

'Well, we must all work together, of course,' the Hermian Ambassador replied. 'But first we must get all the facts about Rama. I have a question for Carlisle Perera. Carlisle, is Rama able to change direction? Or must it remain on its present course? What is its source of energy? Where are its motors? How does Rama move through space?'

Doctor Perera smiled.

'I have an idea about that,' he said. 'Rama has no rocket motors, as far as we know. And Commander Norton has not seen any motors of any kind, inside or outside Rama. But he has not explored the southern end of Rama. We have photos of that end, but they are all we have.'

'Then what's your answer to my question?' the Hermian Ambassador asked quietly.

'I think that Rama has a Space Drive,' Perera replied. 'As you all know, our spaceships are powered by rocket propulsion[57]. The power of the external rockets pushes a spaceship up from the surface of a planet, and into an orbit around it. To escape from this orbit, the spaceship has to reach a very high speed. After that, the ship moves on by the power of its own internal motors.

'There are no rockets on Rama,' Perera went on. 'But that huge cylinder can move very, very fast. It can move fast enough to escape the gravity of planets. So something much stronger than a planet's gravitational pull[58] is powering Rama. We have often thought about something like this. We call this idea a Space Drive. Our scientists have been trying to design a Space Drive for two centuries.'

'There is something else that I don't understand,' someone said. 'If Rama can increase its speed suddenly to escape from an orbit, everything inside the cylinder must be fixed in some way. But we have been told about a sea inside Rama. When Rama changes speed, what happens to the water in the Cylindrical Sea? How does it stay where the explorers have seen it? Why doesn't the water cover all of the southern part of the cylinder?'

Carlisle Perera did not reply immediately. He was thinking. Suddenly he shouted, 'Of course! The very high cliff at the southern side of the Sea! That's the answer! You've all seen the high cliff on the photos. It is almost half a kilometre high. It must be just high enough to hold back the water when Rama accelerates to its full speed. Rama is very well designed. I think that it can go anywhere that the Ramans want it to go. We can't stop it.'

'Thank you, Carlisle,' the Hermian Ambassador said. 'You have given us all a lot to think about. I'm sure now that Commander Norton must cross the Cylindrical Sea. He must explore the southern part of Rama.'

Dr Bose, the Ambassador for Mars spoke. 'Yes, you're right,' he said. 'Norton is already building a boat. We'll send him a message immediately.'

———

Norton and his crew had returned to the interior of Rama. The storm had ended and the strange, enormous world was safe again. The light from the six long grooves had changed colour. The light was no longer a blue colour, it was a soft yellow.

This time, the first expedition was made by Mercer, Calvert and Myron. They had all explored inside Rama before, but then it had been cold and dark. Now they were moving in a warm, bright world.

This expedition was going to be short. Norton only wanted the three men to check that more teams could safely go further towards the south.

There were now many clouds in the interior of Rama. But the clouds were all near the wall of the cylinder. The central area – the area around the axis – was completely clear.

The three men went down Alpha Ladder and got ready to move onto the first part of Alpha Stairway. Mercer checked his breathing equipment. Then he checked the air around him.

He smiled and he called Hub Control.

'I have good news, Commander,' he told Norton. 'There's enough oxygen for us to breathe here now. And the air contains more moisture[59] than before. The air here is now like the air in a hot, wet country on Earth on a summer evening. This time, we can go on from the Inner Terrace without our breathing equipment. We'll be able to move more quickly.'

The three men started their journey down the handrail. At first, the air around them was clear. But then they entered a thick white mist.

The mist was so thick that they couldn't see anything further than a metre from them. Mercer, who was in front, stopped suddenly. The others almost knocked him off the rail as they tried to stop.

'We must go more slowly,' Mercer said. 'I might have to stop again. I can't see anything in front of me now.'

The three men went on more carefully. At Level Five, the explorers came out of the mist and Mercer spoke.

'Look at the Cylindrical Sea,' he said. He seemed puzzled. 'The water was blue before. Now it's bright green! What's happening to it?'

'Life is coming to the water,' Calvert replied. 'The chemicals in the water have reacted with[60] the light inside Rama. That's where the extra oxygen in the air has come from. The green colour comes from tiny plants in the water. This is the next stage of development on Rama. This is how life began on Earth, but on Earth it happened over millions of years. On Rama, life has developed in 48 hours!'

8

New York

The next expedition was to the 'city' of New York, on its island in the Cylindrical Sea. *Endeavour's* engineers had made a small flat boat to carry a team of explorers across the sea to the island. They called the boat, *Resolution*. It was made from storage drums[61], held together by a metal frame. The boat had a small motor and it was just large enough to carry four people. Norton, Mercer and Calvert were members of the team. The fourth member was Sergeant Ruby Barnes.

The island was about five kilometres from the northern shore of the Sea. The short journey across the green water was both frightening and exciting. The strange Cylindrical Sea curved up on either side of the explorers, and over their heads. The water above them did not, and could not, fall. But it was still a terrifying sight.

Laura Ernst had told the explorers that the Cylindrical Sea was now full of single-cell life-forms[62]. These had changed the Sea's colour, which was now green. The tiny creatures in the Sea lived for only a short time. When they died, the chemicals in their bodies became part of the water. Doctor Ernst had also told the explorers that it would be dangerous to swallow more than a few drops of Rama's sea water.

After travelling for 20 minutes, the team could see some details of the buildings of New York quite clearly. Some of the buildings were hundreds of metres high. Norton knew, from the photos which they had taken from the Hub, that there were three groups of buildings on the long, narrow island. The three groups were in a row and each group was circular. Each circular group was divided into three areas, like slices of a round cake. So there were nine areas, all the same size. And each of these nine areas contained a similar group of buildings – towers, domes, spheres and walkways[63].

'Everything here is made in threes,' Norton said. 'That will make our exploration easier. We'll only have to look at one area of New York. The other eight areas will be exactly the same.'

Norton was the first member of the team to land on the island. The others waited in the boat. Near the middle group of buildings, a stairway led up from the water to the top of the outer wall of the city. Norton climbed the steps carefully. The top of the wall was about ten metres wide. For a minute, Norton stood here looking down at the ground level of the city, 20 metres below him. Many stairways and ramps[64] led down from the wall to this ground level. But nothing was moving on them. And nothing was moving in the streets of the city. Everything was quiet.

'Come up and join me,' Norton called to the others. 'We'll start exploring immediately.'

New York's main streets were concentric circles. The circular streets of each of the three groups of buildings were linked by narrower, straight streets – like the spokes of a wheel. There were three of these spokes for each group.

–––––

An hour later, Norton was sure about one thing. This place wasn't a city. But what was it?

'Does anyone want to make a guess about this place?' he asked the others, as they walked along one of the curved streets. 'If New York isn't a city, what is it? Is it a factory? But if it's a factory, what is made here, and what is it made from? And who makes it?'

'Perhaps it *is* a factory,' Mercer said. 'Perhaps the Ramans use the sea water. The water is full of chemicals. But what could the Ramans use them for?'

'Perhaps they use them to make more Ramans,' Calvert said.

But no one laughed. No one wanted to think about that idea.

Norton and his team took photos of everything that they saw. Everything looked clean and new. Everything was completely silent and still.

They reached the southern side of the city and they stood looking out over the water. As they already knew from their photos, the southern shore of the Cylindrical Sea had a very tall cliff. The cliff was about 500 metres high and it looked smooth. Norton could see no stairways or ramps ascending it. How did the Ramans reach the land on that side of the sea? And how could the explorers reach it?

The team left the island and returned to the north shore of the Cylindrical Sea. As they walked up the steps to the Plain, Norton felt unhappy. He had learnt nothing important about Rama or the Ramans that day. Perhaps the southern end of the cylinder – the Southern Hemisphere – was the most important part of this strange world. He wanted to go there. He wanted to find out about the huge spikes. But his crew would have to climb a 500-metre cliff before they could explore the southern part of Rama. And that now seemed impossible. Once again, Norton felt that his mission had failed.

———

Later that day, Commander Norton was sitting in his cabin on *Endeavour*. Someone knocked on the door.

'Come in,' Norton called.

A happy-looking young man came into the room. He was the ship's youngest officer, Lieutenant Jimmy Pak.

'Well, Jimmy, how can I help you?' Norton asked.

'I have an idea that might interest you, Commander,' the young man said. 'I know that you want someone to explore Rama's Southern Hemisphere. I'd like to fly there.'

'How would you fly?' Norton asked. He was puzzled.

'In a sky-bike,' Jimmy replied. 'A sky-bike is small. It would easily go through the airlocks into Rama's interior. And it doesn't need any fuel. There is almost no gravity along Rama's axis. In a sky-bike, I could fly close to the axis most of the way, resting whenever I wanted. When I got beyond the Cylindrical Sea, I could descend to the Plain. Or I could easily fly from the Hub to the South Pole and back again. It would be no problem.'

'Well, it's a clever idea, Jimmy,' Norton said. 'But we haven't got a sky-bike on the mission – have we?'

Jimmy's face turned red.

'I brought my sky-bike with me, as part of my personal luggage, Commander,' he replied. 'I brought it onto the ship in several pieces. I call my bike *Dragonfly*. It's a great machine!' Jimmy looked at Norton's face. 'I'm sorry – I know that I was wrong,' he said. 'But the bike only weighs 20 kilos.'

'Well, Jimmy, you broke an important rule of space travel when you brought your sky-bike onto *Endeavour*,' Norton said. 'No one is allowed to bring large pieces of sports equipment[65] onto a spaceship.' Then he smiled. 'But your bike is the only chance we have of getting some good photos of the Southern Hemisphere. How long will the flight take?'

'About three hours in each direction, if I go right to the South Pole,' Jimmy replied. 'You won't be disappointed with *Dragonfly*, Commander. And you won't be disappointed with me!'

'Well, you can make your journey,' said Norton. 'But you must do it soon. We don't have much more time here!'

———

The pieces of Jimmy's sky-bike were taken through the airlocks to Hub Control. Working very carefully, Jimmy Pak fixed all the pieces together. The sky-bike was fragile – it could be damaged easily. So Jimmy would not allow anybody else to touch it.

Norton watched as Jimmy got inside the strange little machine. The body of *Dragonfly* was a very light frame of metal wire which was covered with very thin, transparent material. The bike's long wings were also covered with this material. The pilot had to sit on a small seat in the centre of the body. He used two pedals to move the bike's propeller[66], and he steered the little machine with a control stick[67] between his knees.

Jimmy began to move the pedals – slowly at first, then faster and faster. The propeller turned, and after a moment, the sky-bike left the Hub.

Dragonfly moved out from the Hub, along the axis of Rama. After a few minutes, Jimmy stopped pedalling. The bike hung in the air, completely still in the zero gravity.

'Is everything OK?' Norton asked Jimmy over his radio.

'The bike is a little difficult to control here,' Jimmy replied. 'I'll fly a little further from the axis for most of the journey. With the help of a little gravity, I'll be able to control *Dragonfly* more easily. I'll return to the axis to rest when I need to. Well, I'm on my way now. Wish me luck, Commander!'

9

Dragonfly's *Flight*

Several members of *Endeavour*'s crew watched Jimmy Pak anxiously as he flew towards the south. But Jimmy passed the northern cliff of the Cylindrical Sea without any problems. He flew out over the water, and the most dangerous part of his journey began. If he fell into the sea, just a mouthful of its water could kill him!

Five minutes after he'd crossed the northern cliff, Jimmy was flying over New York. He flew further from the axis here, so that he could take photos with a small camera.

'These buildings are beautiful,' Jimmy thought. 'But why are they here?'

Fifteen minutes later, Jimmy had crossed the Sea and he was flying over the southern part of the Central Plain.

'How are you feeling, Jimmy?' the Communications Officer at Hub Control asked him. 'Are you getting tired?'

'No, I'm fine,' Jimmy replied. 'How far am I from the South Pole now?'

'About 15 kilometres,' Hub Control answered. 'Don't fly too far from the axis, Jimmy. Be careful. And take lots of short rests.'

'Don't worry,' the young man said. 'I'll be OK. And I'll rest whenever I need to rest.'

Forty minutes after his conversation with Hub Control, Jimmy was entering Rama's Southern Hemisphere. Here at the south end of the cylinder, there were no ladders or stairways. Instead of a 'hub' at the centre of this southern bowl, there was a huge spike. The spike extended out along Rama's axis, and it was more then five kilometres long. In a circle around it, there were six smaller spikes. Each was about half the length of the central one. The outer spikes were joined together, and connected to the central one, by curved buttresses[68]. The spikes looked very strong, but they were beautiful too. They were like the pointed towers of a church or a temple.

Jimmy Pak moved closer to the central spike.

'Tell us what you see, Jimmy,' Hub Control told the young man.

'I'm quite close to the big spike now,' Jimmy replied. 'It looks completely smooth and the point is extremely sharp. At the moment, I'm flying very slowly, just above the spike. But I'm going to use a sticky bomb to pull myself right up to the spike now.'

Jimmy threw a sticky bomb. The bomb flew slowly through the air, leaving a strong, thin cable behind it. The bomb hit the surface of the spike and stuck to it. Then Jimmy pulled himself, and *Dragonfly*, along the cable until he reached the spike. The young man put his hand on its surface.

'Control – the surface feels like glass and it's slightly warm,' Jimmy reported. 'I'm holding a microphone against it now. The microphone is connected to my radio. Can you hear anything?'

Jimmy remained silent for a minute. Then Hub Control replied.

'No, we can't hear anything, Jimmy. Hit the spike with your hand, please. We want to know if it's hollow inside. The sound that you make should tell us that. Then move slowly along the whole length of the spike, towards the South Pole. Take photos of the spike every half-metre. And please look out for anything unusual on its surface.'

'OK,' said Jimmy.

As the young man flew closer to the southern end of Rama, he passed the smaller, outer spikes. Jimmy thought that these spikes looked like tall, thin mountains. But the Ramans must have had a reason for making them. What was the purpose of these strange objects? Jimmy Pak had no ideas about this.

When Jimmy tried to report to Hub Control again, the Communications Officer found it difficult to hear him or speak to him. But at last, Jimmy heard the man's voice.

'Jimmy, something strange is happening,' said Control. 'We are getting an unusual sound from your radio. I'll play it back to you. Listen!'

Jimmy listened. He heard a deep sound, like a very loud heart-beat[69]. The sound became louder then softer every five seconds.

'We think that you are in the middle of some kind of force-field[70] – probably a magnetic field,' Control said. 'The field is very strong and it might be dangerous. Move quickly away from the central spike. Then listen to the sound again. Try to find out where it's coming from.'

Jimmy did what Control had asked him. When he listened to the sound again, it was quieter, but it still frightened him.

'Is this the sound of the motor which powers Rama?' he asked himself.

———

Jimmy pedalled *Dragonfly* back towards the point of the central spike. Hub Control still seemed very far away, but at least he was now on his way back to the Northern Hemisphere.

Jimmy was near the points of the outer spikes when strange things began to happen to him. First his head started to feel very heavy. Then he thought that he felt something touch his hand. When he looked down at it, all the hairs on the skin of his hand were standing up. And he could feel the hairs on his head doing the same thing.

'The air is full of electricity,' Jimmy thought. 'I'm in the middle of an electrical field, not a magnetic one.'

'Hub Control,' Jimmy called. 'There's going to be some kind of storm here at any moment. The outer spikes are sending out electricity. I'm moving away from here as fast as I can!'

As Jimmy finished speaking, he saw flashes of light all around him. They seemed to be dancing on the points of the outer spikes. They were like lines of flame, hundreds of metres

... he saw flashes of light all around him.

long. And suddenly, thunder boomed and crashed.

Jimmy pedalled as fast as he could. If *Dragonfly* broke up now, Jimmy would fall eight kilometres to the cylinder wall – he would be killed.

As he passed the sharp point of the central spike, Jimmy realised that there were other dangers. A strong wind was blowing now, and it was pushing *Dragonfly* from side to side. It was difficult to fly straight. And there was a hissing sound coming from the point of the big spike.

Then suddenly, a huge flash of light filled the air. Long lines of flame shot out from the central spike towards each of the outer ones. And the full power of the electrical storm hit Jimmy.

He just had time to radio a message to Hub Control.

'I'm going to crash!' he shouted. 'One wing of my sky-bike has broken and the other is damaged. The propeller is still working. I'll steer the sky-bike for as long as I can. But I'm in trouble here!'

The watcher at Hub Control could see what was happening to Jimmy through the big telescope. But nobody could help the young man. He was still pedalling strongly, but *Dragonfly* was falling. The machine turned over and over as it fell slowly towards the Central Plain.

Jimmy looked down at the Plain as he fell. The land was divided into big squares of many different colours.

Jimmy still had a little control of his machine. But 100 metres above the Plain, the little sky-bike's right wing broke off completely.

A moment later, *Dragonfly* crashed to the ground.

10

The Fields of Rama

Jimmy Pak woke up with a bad headache, but he was pleased to be alive. He moved his arms and legs carefully. He had no broken bones, but his body felt sore. He opened his eyes, then quickly closed them again. The bright light hurt them.

A few minutes later, as he lay on the ground with his eyes closed, Jimmy heard a strange sound. He turned his head and opened his eyes again. He had a horrible shock.

About five metres from where he was lying, Jimmy saw something that he didn't understand. Was it an animal of some kind? Or was it a machine? Jimmy didn't know. But whatever it was, it seemed to be eating the remains of *Dragonfly*! Jimmy rolled away from the strange thing, very, very slowly. He was afraid that it would see him and attack him. But the thing ignored him completely – it wasn't interested in him.

When he was ten metres from the thing, Jimmy sat up and looked at it more carefully. It had a flat, metallic-looking body. The body was about two metres long and one metre wide. And the thing had six long legs, each with three joints. It also had four long arms with claws on the ends. On the front of its body the thing had big, bright blue eyes and some short arms with tools on the ends.

As he looked more closely, Jimmy saw that the thing was not really eating *Dragonfly*. It was cutting the sky-bike up into small pieces, using its claws. Then it was putting the pieces onto its flat back. And it continued to ignore Jimmy.

'Hub Control,' Jimmy said very quietly into his radio.

The radio still worked. Jimmy heard a voice.

'Jimmy, we're very pleased to hear from you. Are you OK?'

'Yes, I'm OK,' Jimmy replied. 'No bones are broken. But there's something strange here. Look at this.'

As he spoke, he turned his camera towards the thing that

was cutting up his sky-bike. He was lucky. The camera worked too.

'What is it, Jimmy?' Hub Control asked. 'Is it an animal or a machine? Is it some kind of robot?'

'Well, its body seems to be made of metal,' Jimmy answered. And it has eyes – it can see me. But it isn't interested in me – it's ignoring me. And yes, I think it's a robot. I think that it's doing its job. And its job is to clear away rubbish.'

As he was speaking, the thing finished what it was doing. It began to move away. Jimmy stood up and followed it. His food and water had been in the sky-bike. The robot had taken them and Jimmy needed to get them back.

'I might be here for a long time,' he thought. 'I'll need my supplies.'

Jimmy watched the robot carefully for a few moments. He studied the movements of its legs and claws. Then he moved quickly. He ran forward and took his containers of supplies from the thing's back. The robot moved on without stopping.

Jimmy quickly drank some water, then he went on following the robot. The thing was moving towards a wide, round hole in the ground. Jimmy ran past the robot, to the edge of the hole. He looked down into it. There was water in the hole but it was about 500 metres below the ground – at the same level as the Sea at the southern cliff.

'Perhaps the hole is connected with the Cylindrical Sea,' Jimmy thought.

There were three ramps leading down to the water. They were fixed to the sides of the hole. And there were several dark caves or tunnels just above the surface of the water.

A moment later, the robot had arrived at the edge of the hole too. With one quick movement, it shook the pieces of Jimmy's sky-bike off its back. They splashed down into the water, far below. Then the thing turned and started to move towards Jimmy.

'Shall I run or shall I stand still?' Jimmy asked himself.

He decided to stand still. He opened both his hands and held them out in front of him.

'This thing might be intelligent,' he thought. He wanted to show it that he had no weapons. But the robot moved straight past Jimmy and on towards the south. It ignored the young man completely.

Jimmy looked down into the hole again. Something was walking very slowly up one of the ramps. It looked like a large metallic tank with legs. And there was something else, just above the surface of the water. It was spinning round and round, very fast, and Jimmy could not see its shape clearly. He stepped back quickly from the edge of the hole. What were all these creatures? Jimmy started to feel frightened and alone.

'I must get back to the Cylindrical Sea,' the young lieutenant told himself. 'I hope that Commander Norton can come quickly and rescue me from the top of that cliff.'

———

Lieutenant Jimmy Pak was walking slowly and carefully towards the Cylindrical Sea. The electrical storm had finished. Jimmy guessed that the Sea was about three kilometres away. He wanted to see as much as possible of this southern part of Rama.

'I'm probably the only human who will ever walk here,' he thought. He took photos of everything he saw as he walked. 'If I don't get back to the Northern Hemisphere, at least Norton will have my photos for information.'

The ground that Jimmy was walking on was divided into large squares. Every square had a different kind of surface. Some of the surfaces shone like jewels. One was made of twisted wire. Another was made of flat, coloured stones. One square was hard and slippery, and difficult to walk on. The next was soft, like a sponge. Sometimes there were narrow paths between the squares, and Jimmy walked on those. He took photos of everything that he saw and he sent radio messages to the Hub from time to time.

'What do you think about this place? What is it?' he asked Hub Control. 'Am I walking through a Raman art gallery? Or is this some kind of Raman puzzle?'

'We're sorry, Jimmy, we have no ideas about that,' Hub Control answered. 'Just keep walking and sending us photos.'

After half an hour, Jimmy came to a square which looked something like a farmer's field on Earth. It was surrounded by fences made from metal posts and wire. There were three of these fences, one inside another.

'Everything on Rama is made in threes,' Jimmy thought.

There were no gates in the fences, but they were not very high, so Jimmy climbed over them. In the centre of the square, there was a deep hole filled with water. Nothing moved in the water, but Jimmy felt that there was danger in it. He took a photo and climbed back over the fences.

71

After that, Jimmy walked more quickly until he came to the Cylindrical Sea.

———

Jimmy Pak stood at the edge of the tall cliff. The water was 500 metres below him. As there were no new instructions from Hub Control, he decided to walk along the top of the cliff.

He walked on, and soon he had left the different-coloured squares behind him. Now Jimmy was looking at fields of soft soil. The soil was smooth and flat, but nothing was growing in it. Part of the surface of each field was covered by a kind of strong plastic. In some fields, there were poles and wires which climbing plants could have grown on. But there were no plants growing on them. All the fields seemed empty.

Then Jimmy saw a tiny dot of bright colour in the distance. Was there something growing among all these empty, lifeless fields after all? Jimmy decided to find out.

When he got closer to it, Jimmy found that the dot of colour was a plant. It was growing up through a hole in the plastic which covered the field. The plant was about one metre tall and there was a circle of blue-green leaves on its green stem. The leaves looked like the feathers of a bird. At the top of the stem was a brightly-coloured flower, divided into three parts. The flower was made of shining tubes of different colours – blue, green and purple. It was beautiful.

'I'll take this flower back to the scientists,' Jimmy thought. But that was not going to be easy. The rest of the field was full of thin, upright metal poles, standing in small square groups.

Jimmy pushed his way through the poles and reached the beautiful flower. He held the stem and broke the flower from it. As he looked at the flower, the rest of the stem of the plant disappeared into the hole in the plastic cover!

'I've killed the plant,' Jimmy thought. 'But I've picked the only flower on Rama and it's beautiful. I'm pleased that I came here.'

———

Commander Norton had a problem. He had to rescue Jimmy Pak from the southern part of the Central Plain. But the cliff at the southern shore of the Cylindrical Sea was half a kilometre high. There were no stairs or ramps in the cliff. There was no way for anyone to climb up or down it.

Norton had asked the Rama Committee to think of an answer to this problem. It was Dr Perera who thought of the best idea. It was also the simplest idea.

'What do you think of Dr Perera's plan?' Norton asked Karl Mercer. 'Will it work?'

'I think so,' Mercer replied. 'But we won't tell Jimmy about it until we see him.'

———

Jimmy Pak was standing at the top of the cliff. Five hundred metres below him, he could see *Resolution*. The little boat had crossed the Cylindrical Sea again. It had come to rescue him.

Resolution had stopped about 50 metres from the cliff. Suddenly, Jimmy heard Commander Norton's voice on his radio.

'This is the plan, Jimmy,' Norton said. 'It's very simple. You have to jump!'

'I can't jump down 500 metres, Commander. I'll be killed,' Jimmy replied.

'No, you won't be killed, Jimmy,' Norton told him. 'The scientists have thought about this carefully. The gravity here is only half of Earth's gravity. You won't fall as fast as you would on Earth. Now listen carefully —.'

Jimmy listened, and he followed Norton's orders. He took off his shirt and held it above his head. The shirt would work like a parachute[71] when he jumped. He took a deep breath, and he jumped over the edge of the cliff.

Jimmy went into the water, feet-first. He tried not to breathe, or open his eyes as the water closed over his head.

73

Then he started to swim up to the surface, using all his strength. A few moments later, he was being pulled onto *Resolution*. He opened his eyes for a moment and took a deep breath of air as the little boat started on its journey back towards the northern shore.

———

'How are you feeling now, Jimmy?' Commander Norton asked a few minutes later. Norton, Mercer and Sergeant Ruby Barnes were looking down at Lieutenant Pak. They were worried.

'I feel sick,' he replied. 'But I'm OK.'

As Jimmy spoke, there was a flash of light in the sky to the south. Suddenly, huge lines of flame shot out of all the spikes in the Southern Hemisphere. The fire crackled and roared. This went on for about five minutes, then it stopped. And then the whole world of Rama shook.

'Look up there!' Karl Mercer shouted. He pointed upwards. 'Look at the sky!'

Above their heads, a huge curved wall of water was moving down towards them. Norton knew immediately what had happened. Rama had changed its course slightly and the change had caused a great wave in the Cylindrical Sea.

'Hold on to the boat very tightly!' he shouted.

But as the four explorers watched the huge, powerful wave rushing towards them, it began to get smaller and to break up. The little boat was safe, and it was still moving quickly towards the north.

'There must be something under the surface of the water which is slowing the wave down,' Norton thought.

But then another danger appeared in front of them. Something was rising up out of the water. It was a huge, frightening creature – a monster. It looked like a very large wheel. It had nine arms like spokes, and there were claws at the ends of the spokes. But two of the monster's arms were broken. At the creature's 'hub' there were three large eyes. One of the eyes was open, but the other two were closed. The monster had been damaged by the huge wave.

As the crew on *Resolution* watched in horror, two smaller creatures came to the surface of the water. They had claws too. They swam round the huge broken monster, using their claws to cut it into pieces.

'That's what happened to *Dragonfly*,' Jimmy told the others. 'But what a terrible smell! That monster isn't a machine or a robot – it's a living creature. Those other creatures are cutting it up while it's still alive. That's horrible!'

'This sea is not a good place for us to be now,' Norton said.

Nobody spoke again until they reached the northern shore. The little boat's crew climbed up the stairway in the cliff, leaving *Resolution* in the water. They were all worried. Rama was awake now. It was becoming more and more dangerous for the explorers from *Endeavour*!

11

Spiders

The big telescope at Hub Control was being used all the time. Members of *Endeavour*'s crew carefully watched every part of Rama. And someone was always guarding Alpha Camp, the camp at the end of Alpha Stairway.

The first Raman 'Spider' appeared at Alpha Camp one evening. It came within ten metres of the camp before anyone saw it.

The creature's body was a sphere, about 20 centimetres in diameter, and there were three round eyes in the body. The creature had three long thin legs, like whips. It was able to move at great speed, spinning round and round on these three thin legs.

This 'Spider', as the explorers immediately named it, spun around the camp. It checked all the explorers' equipment. It examined everything except the people. The Spider seemed to have no interest in humans.

'I wish that I could catch that creature and study it,' Dr Ernst said. But as she spoke, the Spider spun away quickly, up the stairway towards the Hub.

Commander Norton called Hub Control on his radio.

'Hub Control, you might get a visitor soon,' he said. Then he gave a careful description of the creature. 'After this, anything might happen,' he went on. 'Rama is awake now and we might get visitors at any time. Some of them might be dangerous. If you see one of the Raman creatures, make a report about it, but don't harm it. We don't want to start a war! Everyone must report anything strange that they see. Please pass this message to all the explorers on the Plain. Tell them about the Spider. Ask for reports. I want to know what's happening everywhere.'

Reports soon came in from exploration teams at London, Rome, Tokyo and other places on the Central Plain. Nothing strange had been seen yet.

———

Within a few hours, there were hundreds of Spiders. They were moving all over the Plain. They were seen on the south side of the Cylindrical Sea, as well as on the north side. But no Spiders were seen on the island of New York.

The Spiders visited all the explorers' camps and they examined all the equipment in them. But they never visited the same place twice and they ignored the humans.

Then one of the Spiders fell from a terrace of the Northern Hemisphere. It lay on the ground near Alpha Camp. It didn't move. The Spider was dead – if it had ever been a living being. This was Laura Ernst's chance to study one of Rama's strange creatures.

*Within a few hours, there were hundreds of Spiders.
They were moving all over the Plain.*

REPORT BY DR LAURA ERNST

To: Commander W.T. Norton and the Rama Committee
Subject of the Report – The Raman Spiders

....

I have examined one of these creatures and I have made the following decisions about them:

1 The Spiders are living creatures. But the chemistry[72] of their bodies is different from a human's chemistry. Their bodies contain many metallic compounds.

2 The Spiders cannot eat, breathe or reproduce themselves. Animals do all these things, so the Spiders are not animals.

3 The creatures have quite large brains and very good eyesight – they can see very well.

4 Internally, three-quarters of a spider's body is made up from large cells which form kinds of electric batteries. These batteries supply all the energy that the creatures need. The Spider which I examined gave me an electric shock when I first cut it open, even though it was dead.

5 These creatures have only one purpose – they collect information. That is all that the Spiders do and that is all that they are able to do.

I must add a note about the other Raman creatures that we have seen. Each kind of creature has been designed to do one thing, and only one thing. All these Raman creatures are robots, but they are also living beings. In our worlds, we do not have living robots. For that reason, we do not understand these Raman creatures very well. Rama is a kind of spaceship, so these creatures may be part of its crew. But I am sure that we have not met the real Ramans yet. They were the makers of this strange, amazing world. If we do meet the real Ramans, we must be very careful. They will be far more intelligent than us.

Dr Laura Ernst

12

The Committee

The Hermian Ambassador was not at the next meeting of the Rama Committee. And there was no message from anyone on Mercury.

Dr Bose, the Ambassador for Mars, was in charge of the meeting. He spoke first.

'We've all studied Commander Norton's latest reports from Rama,' he said. 'There are many things for us to discuss. But before we begin, two of our members want to make statements to the Committee. Professor Davidson will speak first.'

The astronomer thanked Dr Bose, and began to speak to the Committee members.

'I've been studying Rama's movements very carefully for the last few days,' Olaf Davidson said. 'The results are rather frightening. Let me explain what I have discovered.

'We've all seen the photos of the electrical display – the fire that flashed between the spikes at Rama's South Pole. One of Norton's crew recorded the powerful forcefield around the spikes while it was happening. At first, we thought that we were seeing something like an electrical storm. But now I've discovered that while that display was happening, Rama's speed of rotation was changing.

'That change used a huge amount of energy,' the astronomer went on. 'I believe that the display which Norton's team saw inside Rama was a result of that energy. So the change in the speed of rotation was not an accident. Somebody or something made it happen!

'I no longer believe that Rama is planning to fly past the Sun and on towards other stars. I now believe that Rama is planning to go into orbit around the Sun.

'Commander Norton must be warned about this. He and his crew are in great danger. If they are inside Rama when it goes into this orbit, the Sun's heat will quickly kill them. Norton must take his people back to *Endeavour*, and he must get his ship as far away from Rama as possible. He must go now!'

'Thank you for those words, Professor,' said the Ambassador for Mars. 'And now Sir Lewis Sands, our historian of science, wants to speak to the Committee.'

'I also have something to say about that change in Rama's speed of rotation,' Dennis Solomons began. 'Professor Davidson will probably not agree with what I have to say. He himself told us that a huge amount of energy was needed to make the change. I agree with that. And I agree that the electrical display which Norton's team saw was caused by that energy. But where did that energy come from? Rama has no rocket motors – we know that. There is only one possibility, and we have talked about it before. Dr Perera told us about it. This spaceship,

Rama, *must* have a Space Drive!'

Olaf Davidson laughed and shook his head.

'The idea of a Space Drive is against everything that we know about the science of physics,' he said. 'A Space Drive, if it existed, would be a kind of motor without fuel. But a spaceship can only move in one direction because its rockets are pushing out hot gases in the opposite direction – we all know that! And the rockets make these hot gases by burning fuel. Every spaceship must be powered by something like that. It must use some kind of fuel.'

'But a Space Drive would not need anything that *we* think of as fuel,' Solomons replied. 'We don't know how a Space Drive would work. But we can say that Rama must have a Space Drive because there is no other explanation for its movement. Perhaps it uses magnetic fields. Perhaps it uses something that

we cannot understand.

'But please listen to me, all of you,' Solomons went on. 'Something is moving Rama at a very great speed. It is true that we don't understand what this is. But what *do* we understand about Rama? We understand very little about it! Professor Davidson is trying to understand Rama by thinking about the things that we already have in our Solar System. But Rama has come from a place where the science of physics is different from the science that we know. There is nothing that we can do to control Rama!'

————

Sergeant Pieter Rousseau was looking through Hub Control's powerful telescope. Rousseau had a new job now – he was Chief Biot Watcher!

A 'biot' was the name which the explorers had given to the creatures – the biological robots – that they had seen on Rama. These creatures were living beings. They each had one kind of job to do, and they did it well. Were the creatures intelligent? Perhaps they were. But perhaps they had been designed by very intelligent beings and they had no intelligence themselves.

At first, there had been hundreds of Spiders rushing around Rama. But after a few days, they had all disappeared. They had been replaced by different creatures. Some of these new biots cleaned the glass-like surfaces of Rama's internal lights. Rousseau called these creatures, the Window Cleaners. He had enjoyed watching them moving along the whole length of Rama's six 'suns'.

Then there were the Scavengers. These biots were like the strange creature which had destroyed Jimmy Pak's sky-bike. Their job was to collect any small objects which they found and to drop these objects into the Sea. Bigger creatures appeared to move larger pieces of 'rubbish'. And other biots lived in the Sea and broke up whatever things the Scavengers dropped into it. These sea-creatures had 'eaten' *Resolution*, which Norton had left, tied to a stairway of the northern cliff. Rousseau called the sea-creatures 'Sharks'.

Pieter Rousseau spent many hours watching the biots. He photographed and catalogued all of them. He was busy and happy. He hoped that he would stay on Rama for many more days.

13

The Hermians Make Their Own Plans

Commander William Norton was at Alpha Camp. He was worried. He had just received a message from Earth.

From: Space Survey Headquarters
To: Commander W.T. Norton.

TOP SECRET – PLEASE DELETE THIS MESSAGE AFTER READING IT

....

Spaceguard has reported that an armed missile[73] was launched from Mercury, between ten and twelve days ago. The missile is moving at very high speed. It will hit Rama if Rama does not change its course. You must leave Rama now.

Commander-in-Chief

Norton did not want to believe what he was reading. Why was Mercury launching an armed missile at Rama? What were the Hermians trying to do? What would happen to Rama now?

———

Three days later, Norton's questions had still not been answered. But by that time, the Hermian missile was flying only 50 kilometres from Rama. It stayed at that distance while cameras on the missile sent photos of Rama back to Mercury. At the same time, *Endeavour*'s cameras sent photos of the missile back to the Space Survey Headquarters. The leaders of Mercury had remained silent. Norton knew that he and his crew would have to leave Rama soon, but he wanted to stay on the cylinder as long as possible.

At last, Mercury sent a message to the United Planets Organisation. The message said that in three hours' time, the Hermian Ambassador would speak to the organisation's General Assembly[74]. This message was sent on to Norton.

Norton could not guess what the Hermian Ambassador was going to say. Hermians were surprising! Norton had visited Mercury, but he'd never wanted to live there. He had several Hermian friends, but he didn't know them very well. No one who was born on Mercury had ever visited Earth – the gravity there was too strong for their bodies. So Hermians were very different from the other people of the Solar System. Hermians liked to work alone.

REPORT

From: Commander-in-Chief of the Space Survey
To: Commander W.T. Norton of *Endeavour*

....

The General Assembly of the United Planets will meet on Luna at 14.00 hours – Earth time. You and your crew will be able to listen to the discussion. You may then have to make an immediate decision.

We have studied your photos and we now have the following information about the missile from Mercury. It is armed with a powerful bomb. If the bomb explodes close to the thinnest part of Rama's wall, it could break Rama into pieces. We believe that the Hermians will give you time to leave Rama before they make the bomb explode. But until you are very far from Rama, you will be in great danger. If the bomb explodes and Rama breaks up, huge pieces of

84

the cylinder will be spinning through space at very high speed. When you leave Rama, fly away from it in the direction of its axis. It is unlikely that any pieces of the broken cylinder will hit you if you stay on that course. The decision about when to leave is one that you must make yourself.

Commander-in-Chief

At the General Assembly meeting of the United Planets on Luna, everyone was very quiet as the Hermian Ambassador stood up and started to speak.

'I must begin with a short report about the danger to the Solar System at the present time,' he said. 'This is the situation. The spaceship Rama was first reported more than a year ago. It was then far away from any of us, beyond Jupiter. At first, everybody thought that Rama was a natural object – perhaps a huge asteroid. When we all understood the truth, the spaceship *Endeavour* was ordered to rendezvous with Rama. It did this, and we all want to thank Commander William Norton for the way that he has completed his difficult and dangerous mission.

'We all studied his reports,' the Ambassador continued. 'Rama seemed to be a dead, empty world. That didn't surprise us. Rama's journey through space had already taken many hundreds of thousands of years. No living being can stay alive for so long a time. We believed that Rama was not a problem for any of us in the Solar System.

'Then our astronomers realised something very important. Rama had been pointed directly at the Sun. We realised then – almost too late – that Rama's course was not an accident. Its course had been planned very carefully.

'We now know the truth. Living creatures do exist on Rama. Commander Norton and his crew have seen them and studied them. And these creatures are not many centuries old – they were made recently. We now believe that the designs for these creatures were stored inside Rama. And at the right time, the designs were used to make these "biots", as Norton's crew calls them. The chemicals which were used to build the biots were in the water of the Cylindrical Sea. So Rama is a living world. We don't know what kind of beings the Ramans are. But their world has entered our Solar System, and that was not an accident. It is what the Ramans had planned!

'Rama has already changed its course once. In a few days, if it stays on its present course, it will be at its closest point to the Sun. When it reaches that point, Rama may change its course again and go into orbit round the Sun. Then it will be like a new planet in the Solar System. And that will be dangerous to us! The Ramans' knowledge of science is hundreds of years – perhaps thousands of years – ahead of our own. So what do the Ramans want from us?

'We Hermians believe that Rama has come to destroy us!' the Ambassador went on angrily. 'On Earth, there is a very successful insect called the termite. Termites live together in colonies. In each colony, there are groups of termites with special jobs. Some termites carry things from one place to another. Some termites are builders, some are farmers, and some are soldiers. The biots on Rama remind me of termites.

'On Earth, humans and termites live in the same places. But they do not understand each other, or work together. It is possible that, one day in the future, termites will destroy humans. They could take over the Earth.

'We know nothing about the Ramans,' the Ambassador said more quietly now. 'We don't know why they sent their spaceship to our Solar System. But we Hermians don't trust them. We think that they want to take over our worlds. We think that they want to destroy all human life. We may be wrong, but we can't take any risks. We, the people of Mercury, have decided to protect ourselves. We have sent an armed missile to rendezvous with Rama. If Rama goes into orbit around the Sun, we will destroy it.

'We don't want to attack Rama, but we will if we have to,' the Ambassador said. 'We will make our decision in the next few days. And we will not ask the permission of the members of this Assembly. We will give Commander Norton time to escape. He and his crew must be ready to leave Rama one hour after our decision is made. He must be told this now. That is all I have to say.'

14

Rodrigo's Mission

Commander Norton and his crew had all returned to Endeavour to listen to the Hermian Ambassador's words.

Were the Ramans a danger to the people of the United Planets? William Norton didn't really believe that they were, and neither did most of his crew. They had explored Rama. They had felt its huge power and they had seen its beauty.

Rama was the Solar System's first visitor from deep space. No one knew why it had come, but it had done no harm. There was no reason to destroy it.

Norton was resting in his cabin when Boris Rodrigo came to see him.

'What do you think about the Hermian Ambassador's fears, Boris?' Norton asked. 'Is he right? What does your religion tell you about situations like this one?'

'I believe that this situation has happened before,' Rodrigo replied seriously. 'I believe that the knowledge which we call religion first came to Earth from the stars. This religion tried to teach humans about good and evil, and about how to choose between them. But people did not learn, and terrible things happened to them. Now Rama has come to help us. It has come to help all good men and women. It has come to save them from evil. The Hermians are wrong – they are very wrong! They must not destroy Rama. Someone must stop them!'

Norton smiled. He knew Rodrigo well.

'What is your suggestion, Boris?' he asked.

'Commander,' Rodrigo replied. 'The bomb that the Hermian missile is carrying must not explode. It will not explode. I'm going to stop that happening!'

'How do you plan to do that, Lieutenant?'

'That's very simple Commander. I'll take the shuttle[75] and I'll make a short journey in space. I'll visit the missile and I'll disarm it. I'll cut the power cables which connect the bomb to the missile.'

'But the Hermians will see you,' Norton said. 'There are cameras on the missile. The Hermians will make their bomb explode before you get near it.'

'If I'm quick, they won't be able to stop me,' Boris replied. 'The pictures from their cameras will take about ten minutes to reach Mercury. I can disarm the missile in a few minutes. By the time the Hermians see me approaching their missile, it will be too late. I shall have finished my job.'

'That sounds like a good plan, Boris,' Norton said. 'And I agree with you about the Hermians. But I'm in charge of this mission and the decision must be mine. I need some time to think about this. Please leave me alone now.'

Norton sat alone in his cabin for some time. Then he sent a message. He asked Lieutenant Rodrigo to come to see him again.

————

Boris was alone in *Endeavour*'s small space shuttle. He was now 25 kilometres from Rama, and half-way to the Hermian missile. The complete journey would only take four minutes. Boris believed that he could cut all the missile's external power cables in about six minutes. He would have just enough time to complete his mission before the Hermians saw the first pictures of him.

Boris looked back at *Endeavour*. The spaceship had moved up from its landing-place between the airlocks at the north end of the huge cylinder. By the time that Boris had reached the missile, Norton would have moved the ship to the opposite side of Rama. Rama would then be between the missile and *Endeavour*. Norton and his crew would be out of danger there.

The missile was shining very brightly in the strong sunlight. As his shuttle got nearer to the missile, Boris could see its cameras. He knew that they were sending photos of him back to Mercury. But they would arrive too late!

The missile was about ten metres long and three metres wide. The bomb was attached to one end of it. Two cables extended from the bomb along the sides of the missile, then disappeared inside it. Boris hoped that, when he had cut these cables, the bomb would be disarmed.

The shuttle moved gently up to the missile and Boris quickly fastened it to the frame which held the bomb. He got out of the shuttle. Moving very slowly in his thick spacesuit, he climbed onto the missile's side. He cut through the first cable easily, then he moved towards the second one. But at that moment, the missile started to shake. The missile was changing its course. It was getting ready to attack Rama.

———

A few minutes before Boris began cutting the bomb's power cables, Norton had received a message from Mercury.

> You have one hour to leave Rama. Please leave the area at full speed. Please answer this message as soon as possible.

Commander Norton was surprised at first, then he was very angry.

'Why have the Hermians decided to attack Rama now?' he

asked himself. 'Rama's course hasn't changed again. But it's too late to stop Boris's mission. And it will take me more than an hour to get *Endeavour* out of this area.'

Norton didn't reply to the message, and ten minutes later another one arrived. It was the same as the first one.

'The Hermians must have seen the pictures of Boris by now,' Norton thought. 'I hope that he can finish his work and get away from that missile in time. I won't answer the Hermians' message until I know that Boris is returning to *Endeavour*.'

Boris could feel the missile shaking as it changed its course. When it was pointing straight at the middle of Rama's cylindrical wall, it began to move forward. Boris was very angry, but he continued working. In a few more moments, he had cut the second cable.

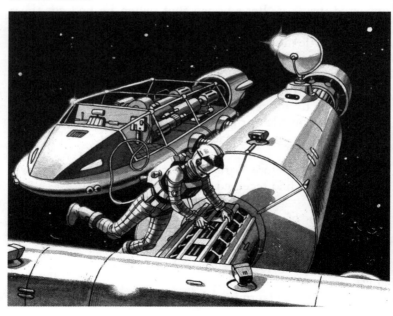

He hoped that now the bomb could not explode. But the Hermians could still send the missile crashing into Rama. Boris knew how he could stop that happening, and he still had time to do it. He crawled along the missile until he reached its radio antenna[76]. He cut the antenna's cable. Now the Hermians had no control over their missile at all.

Boris quickly moved back into the shuttle. He used the shuttle to push the front end of the missile round, so that it pointed away from Rama. Soon, he had changed its direction completely. Now the missile would fly on until it ran out of fuel somewhere far away in deep space.

Boris's mission had been a complete success. He started his journey back to *Endeavour*.

15

The Temple of Glass

Rama was safe from the missile now, but the enormous cylinder was still flying nearer and nearer to the Sun. Rama's walls were very thick, and they could protect the interior from the Sun's heat for many more days. But *Endeavour*, which had landed between Rama's northern airlocks again, would soon be in danger. In two days' time, Norton would have to leave Rama. If he did not, *Endeavour* would be destroyed by the Sun's heat.

Norton had plans for those two days. He wanted to go into Rama's interior again. He talked to Karl Mercer about his plans.

'On this expedition, I want to get into some of the buildings,' Norton said. 'We'll have to cut through their walls. I didn't want to do that before, but we must find out some more of Rama's secrets before we leave.'

'Will the biots try to stop us?' Mercer asked. 'Some of them are very large. They could be dangerous.'

'I don't think that they'll harm us,' Norton replied. 'They don't seem to be interested in us. And now I think that I understand why. It's because we breathe oxygen. The Ramans breathe oxygen too – we know that from the air inside the cylinder. The biots probably can't see any difference between one kind of oxygen-breather and another. They probably think that we are Ramans! That's why they ignore us!

'We'll cut into some of the buildings in London, because that is the nearest city to a stairway,' Norton went on. 'London is close to the end of Beta Stairway. If we have to leave Rama very quickly, it will be good to be close to a stairway.'

———

Nothing had changed in London. Its streets were empty and silent. The walls of its long, high buildings were completely smooth. There were no openings of any kind.

A team of four men from *Endeavour* moved quickly through the streets. Norton, Mercer, Myron and Calvert were worried. Was something watching them? All the time, they were expecting to hear an alarm that would warn the Ramans about them. But the explorers saw nothing unusual and they heard nothing unusual. They prepared their equipment and they started work.

Sergeant Myron picked up his laser cutter. Soon, a powerful laser beam was cutting through the wall of one of the buildings. In a few minutes, Myron had cut a large hole in the wall. And there were still no alarms or warnings.

Norton was the first man to enter the building. He walked through the hole and shone his flashlight around him. He was standing between some tall columns. And there were columns as far as he could see – rows and rows of tall, thin cylinders.

These columns extended from the floor to the ceiling and they were about one metre wide. They were made of something that looked like glass.

'This is very pretty,' Mercer said as he joined Norton inside the building. 'Is this place some kind of Raman church or a temple?'

Mercer began to walk beside a row of columns, looking carefully at each one.

'These columns are hollow, but they aren't empty,' he called to Norton. 'If you stand in the right place, you can see inside them. Try it yourself.'

The other two explorers had now entered the building. All four men walked slowly round dozens of the columns, until they could see what was inside each one. Each column seemed to contain an object, and each object was different.

'Are they real things or are they holograms[77]?' Joe Calvert asked.

'I think that they're real things,' said Norton. 'We must be in a museum. But it's a strange one! There are small machines, containers, tools, all mixed together with plates, knives, cups and things like that.'

The four men began to take photos. As they worked, Norton had another idea.

'No! This isn't a museum,' he said. 'It's a catalogue. It's an illustrated list of all the things that the Ramans know about. These are designs for things that they might want to make.'

'Yes, I understand what you mean,' Mercer said. 'When the Ramans want a knife, or a hammer, they make one using a design from this place.'

'Perhaps they do the same thing when they want biots,' Calvert said. 'Perhaps biots are not made until they are wanted. We know that each kind of biot is made for one kind of job.'

Mercer moved along another row of columns. 'Come here, everyone,' he called. 'Look at this!'

Mercer was standing by a column which was wider than the first ones that they had seen – it was about two metres wide. Inside the column there was a kind of harness[78]. The harness was made for a creature that stood upright on legs, but was much taller than a human.

The harness included two belts. The lower belt was narrow, the one above it was much wider. The upper and lower belts were joined by straps. There were three openings on the upper belt. Perhaps these were for a creature's arms – three of them! All over the harness there were pockets and loops. These contained tools of many kinds and strange black boxes.

'Do you think that this was made for a Raman?' Norton asked the others.

'Well, it was made for a creature which was more than two and a half metres tall,' Mercer replied. 'And we think that the Ramans must be bigger than us. We thought that when we first saw the size of the steps of the stairways.'

'If this harness was made for a Raman, the Ramans must have three arms,' said Joe Calvert. 'And they probably have three legs too. The Spiders had three legs and three eyes. The monster in the sea had three eyes too. It had nine legs – three threes! The Ramans probably make their biots to be like themselves in some ways.'

'Do you think that the Ramans are watching us now?' Mercer asked quietly.

'I don't think so,' said Norton sadly. 'We aren't intelligent enough for the Ramans to care about.'

At that moment, Norton got a message from Hub Control.

'Commander, you must all come back to the Hub quickly!' said the voice.

'What's the problem? Have the biots returned?' Norton asked.

'No. It's something more serious than that,' the voice replied. 'All the lights are fading.'

As the four explorers quickly left the building, Norton looked around him. The six 'suns' of Rama were still shining, but their light was much weaker than it had been.

'OK,' said Norton. 'This is the end of our mission. We're

'Do you think that the Ramans are watching us now?'

going home. Leave all the equipment here. We must get back to Beta Stairway quickly. It's only four kilometres away, but we must hurry. We don't know what's going to happen next.'

As the explorers walked quickly towards Beta Stairway, Rama shook gently for a few seconds.

'What's happening?' Norton asked Hub Control.

'We think that Rama is changing its course again, Commander,' Control replied.

Then there was a second movement. This one was more powerful.

'Rama must be going into orbit,' Norton told Control. 'I didn't expect that to happen so soon. Get *Endeavour* ready. We must leave as soon as we can.'

The interior of Rama was now much darker. The four men had to use their flashlights. Then the big searchlight was switched on at Hub Control. Now its beam showed the explorers the way to Beta Stairway.

The first part of the climb was very difficult. There was no time to rest at each terrace. But after Level Three, the pull of gravity was less strong. The ascent became easier, and Norton and his team felt happier.

Suddenly they heard a strange whistling sound. At first it was loud and clear. Then it became quieter. Then it grew louder again, then quieter. It was some kind of alarm. Who or what was it for?

But suddenly, round balls of flashing light began to move along the six darkening suns in the cylinder wall. The balls of light were moving from the North and South Poles, towards the Cylindrical Sea. It was a message to everything that had been made on Rama.

'To the Sea! To the Sea!' the message was saying.

'Hub Control, what's happening now?' Norton asked.

'All the biots are moving to the Cylindrical Sea,' Control

replied. 'They're moving faster and faster, from every part of Rama, and they're throwing themselves into the Sea. The creatures that live in the water are destroying them. This is the end of the biots. Please hurry, Commander! If you don't get up here quickly, it may be the end of you too. We mustn't stay here any longer!'

Rama shook again as the explorers completed their ascent. It had turned onto its new course. And soon it would increase its speed – Norton knew that. But before Rama did that, *Endeavour* had to be far away from this strange world.

As the four men reached the Hub, they looked back and saw that everything had changed. The balls of light had gone and the whistling sound had stopped. The strips of light in the wall were very, very weak now. There was mist covering the South Pole. There were big waves in the Cylindrical Sea.

As the rest of the crew helped the explorers into the airlocks, the last light faded inside Rama.

'This is sad,' Norton thought. 'The day is ending in this beautiful, amazing world. Night is coming back to Rama as it gets nearer and nearer to the terrible brightness of the Sun.'

16

The Vast Space Beyond the Solar System

Endeavour was a hundred kilometres away from Rama now. Rama was turning again – everybody could see that. But it was turning very, very slowly. Was it moving into an orbit around the Sun? The scientists of the United Planets were very excited by the cylinder's change of direction. Everyone had a suggestion about the reason for it. But the men and women on *Endeavour* were too tired to care about these suggestions.

Two 'nights' after their escape, Karl Mercer came to Norton's cabin and woke him.

'Rama has stopped turning now, Commander,' he said. 'I think that it's ready to move on.'

A few minutes later, Norton was sitting at *Endeavour*'s controls. The ship was getting too hot and he tried to fly it into Rama's shadow. But suddenly, *Endeavour* started to shake. Norton could not control the spaceship. In a moment, the ship was spinning round and round. Some terrible force-field from Rama was pulling *Endeavour* after the huge cylinder.

At the same time, Rama began to increase its speed. It moved faster and faster, further and further away from *Endeavour*. But what was powering Rama through the sky at such a speed? And what force-field had caught *Endeavour* so that Norton couldn't control the ship?

Norton was very worried. *Endeavour* was now dangerously close to the Sun. But he knew what he had to do. By using the full power of the ship's motors, he flew it out of Rama's force-field.

By the time *Endeavour* was out of danger, Rama was 200,000 kilometres away. And it was moving faster and faster towards the centre of the Solar System – towards the Sun itself! Had the Ramans made a mistake? Was this journey – a journey that perhaps had lasted for a million years – going to end in a huge explosion? Was Rama going to be destroyed by the terrible heat of the Sun?

Everyone had expected that Rama would slow down as it got nearer to the Sun. Everyone had thought that the Sun's gravity would pull Rama into an orbit. Then the huge cylinder would become like another planet in the Solar System. But that was not happening. Rama was moving faster and faster towards the surface of the Sun.

'Rama is going to be destroyed,' Norton said to himself sadly.

Rama was moving faster and faster towards the centre of the Solar System.

'And there is nothing we, or the Ramans, can do about it! Very soon, the cylinder will begin to melt. It will turn to liquid.'

Rama now looked like a tiny bright star. And as Norton watched it, the star became pale. But a moment later, he saw that the cylinder was inside a huge, transparent sphere. And he understood that the huge shining ball was protecting Rama from the Sun's heat.

As the hours passed, the ball changed its shape. At first, it had been round. Then it became long and thin. But Rama was still inside it. And now, something began to change the magnetic field around the Sun. Huge lines of flame were shooting out from the Sun's surface, towards the bubble around Rama. Norton understood that, somehow, Rama was using the Sun's magnetic energy as fuel.

Rama moved faster and faster, then suddenly it changed course again. In a moment, it was free of the pull of the Sun's gravity. Rama flew on and on, at an unbelievable speed, out of the Solar System and towards the vast space beyond it.

———

Commander William Norton never knew whether his mission had succeeded or failed. He and his crew had landed on Rama. They had explored it, and they had all escaped safely from it. But they had failed to understand what the Ramans were, or why they had come.

The Ramans had not visited the Solar System to meet the people who lived there – the Committee knew that now. The Ramans were not interested in humans. They had used the Sun as a power source. And now Rama was travelling on its way to more important places in the Universe.

Norton thought then that the best part of his life was over. He believed that nothing like Rama would ever be seen again.

But the Commander had forgotten one thing —

The Ramans always make things in threes!

Points for Understanding

1

1 In the late twenty-first century, the purpose of Project Spaceguard was to protect the Earth. But in 2131, its purpose has changed. It now protects the Solar System. What is the reason for this change?
2 Asteroids have irregular shapes. How does this fact help astronomers know that they are looking at an asteroid, even when it is very far away?
3 The Spaceguard scientists find out that Rama is hollow. How do they learn this?

2

1 Why has Commander Norton decided to land *Endeavour* at the centre of Rama's north end? Give two reasons.
2 Norton is worried about the landing place that he has chosen. Why?
3 'Do Ramans have hands like us?' Karl Mercer asks. Why does he ask this question?
4 'Perhaps Rama is a tomb,' Norton thinks. Why does he think this?

3

1 'The number three must be important to the Ramans,' Norton tells himself. What things, described in this chapter and in Chapter Two, have made him think this?
2 Norton and his crew have used flares to photograph the interior of Rama. They have photographed something that looks like an island in a sea. They have named this place New York. Why?
3 Doctor Perera says that Rama has been travelling for *at least* 200,000 years. How does he know this?

4

1 When Mercer, Calvert and Myron start to move down Alpha Stairway, Calvert makes a guess about the Ramans. What is his guess and what is his reason for making it?

2 At Level Two, Mercer tells Norton that he can breathe the air. Why is this good news?

5

1 'The thinnest part of Rama's wall is probably the part at the bottom of the Cylindrical Sea,' Dr Perera says. Why does he think this? Make a guess.

2 'This liquid has *never* contained life,' Dr Ernst tells Commander Norton. This sentence should remind you of several things that Norton has said earlier in the story. Write down two sentences which connect with what Dr Ernst is saying here.

6

1 Norton and the crew of *Endeavour* have to leave Rama when the ice starts to break up. The last part of the exploring teams' climb to the Hub is the most difficult part of the journey. Why? Give two reasons.

2 Boris Rodrigo does not think that Rama is in the Solar System by chance. He believes that Rama has been *sent* to the Solar System. Why does he think this? Who does he think sent Rama?

7

1 *Endeavour*'s crew goes back into Rama, and Mercer, Calvert and Myron start to descend to the Plain. What does Mercer find out when they reach the Inner Terrace?

2 When they reach the Plain, the explorers discover something which explains the answer to the previous question. What do they discover?

8

1 Each circular group of buildings in New York is divided into three equal sections by three straight streets. At what angle are these streets to each other?

2 Jimmy doesn't want to fly his sky-bike along Rama's axis. Why not?

9

1 Hub control asks Jimmy Pak to hit the central spike with his hand. Why?

2 'The air is full of electricity,' Jimmy thinks. What makes him think this?

10

1 The robot drops the pieces of *Dragonfly* into a hole. Jimmy Pak thinks, 'Perhaps the hole is connected to the Cylindrical Sea.' Why does he think this?

2 Why does Jimmy take his shirt off before he jumps into the Cylindrical Sea?

11

1 The explorers see some creatures with spherical bodies, three eyes and three long legs. They name the creatures 'Spiders'.
   (a) Is this a good name for the creatures?
   (b) How are these creatures like spiders?
   (c) How are they *different* from spiders?

2 What is a spy? Why is this word a good description of the Spiders? Give two reasons. (Think about the sound of the word as well as its meaning.)

12

1 Why does Olaf Davidson think that Rama is going to go into orbit around the Sun?
2 Why does the crew use the name 'biots' for the Raman creatures?

13

1 People who are born on Mercury cannot travel to every other inhabited part of the Solar System. Why?
2 'What do the Ramans want from us?' the Hermian Ambassador asks the Rama Committee. What does he think they *don't* want? Why does he think this?

14

1 Boris Rodrigo thinks that his plan will work. What fact about radio transmission makes him think this?
2 At what speed does Boris's shuttle fly? Explain how you got your answer.

15

1 The Raman biots always ignore the human visitors. Norton has an idea about why this happens. What is his idea?
2 'Is this place some kind of Raman church or temple?' Mercer asks. Why do you think he asks this question?

16

Everybody's ideas about Rama have been wrong. Explain (a) how the Hermian Ambassador's ideas were wrong and (b) how Boris Rodrigo's ideas were wrong.

Glossary

1   **orbit** (page 4)

when an object in space is *in orbit*, it is moving round and round a larger object. The path which the smaller object flies on is called its *orbit*, and it can also be said to be *following an orbit*. The orbit of the smaller object is controlled by the gravity of the larger object (see page 6) unless the smaller object has its own power – e.g. a spaceship. *Orbit* can also be used as a verb. Satellites orbit the Earth, the Earth orbits the Sun, etc.

2   **degree** (page 4)

this word has several different meanings in English. A *degree* is a qualification that you get when you successfully complete a course at a university. But the word degree is often used to mean a small part of something, especially something which is divided into equal parts. Two meanings of this kind appear in this book. (a) *Degrees of temperature* – 5,5000°C for example. This is a measurement of how hot or cold a thing or place is. (b) *Degrees of a circle* – The circumference of a circle is divided into 360 equal parts, or degrees. If you divide the area of a circle into three equal parts with lines from the centre to the circumference, the lines are 120 degrees apart. This can be written as 120°. If the area is divided into four, the lines are 90° apart. (See the illustration on page 10.)

3   **physics** (page 4)

the science that includes knowledge about different kinds of energy – heat, light, electricity, etc.

4   **missions** (page 5)

if you decide to travel somewhere to do something, or find out about something, you are on a *mission*.

5   **contract** (page 6)

when something grows smaller in every dimension, it *contracts*. When it grows larger, it *expands*. NOTE: this verb is pronounced con-**tract**.

6   **spin** (page 6)

something which *spins*, turns round and round very quickly. Another verb with nearly the same meaning is *rotate*, but things can rotate slowly.

7   **asteroids** (page 6)

large pieces of rock which fly through space. There are many *asteroids* between Mars and Jupiter.

8   *axis* (page 6)
    when something spins or rotates, the imaginary line which it rotates around is called its *axis*. (See the illustration on page 10.)
9   *grooves* (page 9)
    lines which are cut into a flat surface.
10 *astronomer* (page 12)
    a scientist who studies the stars and planets in space.
11 *archeologist* (page 12)
    a scientist who studies objects and buildings from the past, to find out about the people who made them.
12 *biologist* (page 12)
    a scientist who studies living things – animals and plants.
13 *anthropologist* (page 12)
    a scientist who studies the way that people behave.
14 *Ambassador* (page 12)
    today, an *ambassador* is the person who speaks for, or *represents*, the government of one country in another country – e.g. the British Ambassador to Spain. In this story, ambassadors represent the different planets and moons of the Solar System.
15 *deep space* (page 13)
    in this book, *deep space* means all the areas of space which are beyond the Solar System.
16 *meteorites* (page 13)
    pieces of rock from space which have fallen on the surface of the Earth.
17 *extinction* (page 13)
    when every one of a particular kind of animal has died, so that no more of them can ever be born, then that animal is *extinct*. The process is called the *extinction* of that animal.
18 *plain* (page 14)
    a large flat area of ground, with no valleys, hills or mountains.
19 *tracked and catalogued* (page 15)
    if you watch something which is moving and you make notes about its movement, you are *tracking* that thing. If you make a list of many things of the same kind, you are making a *catalogue* of these things. The things have then been *catalogued*.
20 *collapsed star* (page 16)
    a star which has suddenly contracted to a much smaller amount of very dense material. Anything which goes near a *collapsed star* will be pulled into it and destroyed.

106

21 **space-probe** (page 16)

a small spaceship which contains cameras, but has no crew on board. A *space-probe* is sent to an area of space, or to an object in space, which has not been explored before.

22 **transmitted** (page 17)

when radio messages are sent from one place to another, they are *transmitted*. Pictures can be transmitted by radio signals, as well as sounds, and that is what happens here.

23 **cylinder** (page 17)

a cylinder is an object with circular ends and parallel sides.

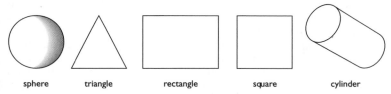

| sphere | triangle | rectangle | square | cylinder |

24 **caught up with** – *to catch up with* (page 18)

if you chase something, when you reach it you have *caught up with* it.

25 **airlock** (page 20)

an entrance into a spaceship. An *airlock* has two doors – an outer door and an inner door, with a space between them. A space traveller must carry air in a tank when moving outside a spaceship, and wear a face-mask or space helmet to breathe the air from the tank. But inside a spaceship, there is air to breathe and the crewmembers do not have to carry air tanks and wear masks or helmets. To enter the ship from outside, a crewmember opens the outside door and moves into the space between the doors. The outside door is then closed before the inside one is opened. This stops the air inside the ship escaping into space. Rama is a very large spaceship, so Norton thinks that it might have an airlock which is big enough to contain a small spaceship.

26 **microphones** (page 20)

pieces of electronic equipment. You speak into a microphone when you want to transmit your voice by radio.

27 **cables** (page 21)

strong ropes made of metal.

28 **EVA** (page 21)

when a crewmember of a spaceship leaves the vehicle (the ship) to do something outside it, this is an *EVA* – an Extra-Vehicular Activity.

29 **expedition** (page 21)

if you travel to a place to explore it, you have gone on an *expedition* to that place.

30 **alarms** (page 21)

an *alarm* is a loud sound which gives a warning that something is wrong.

31 **risks** – *to take risks* (page 22)

if you know that it is dangerous to do something but you do it anyway, you are *taking a risk*.

32 **mobile cameras** (page 24)

cameras which move on wheels or are on, or inside, a machine that can fly. These cameras transmit their pictures by radio.

33 **safety line** (page 25)

a kind of rope or cable used by explorers, climbers and space travellers. One end is fixed to a person who is going to do something dangerous. The other end of the *safety line* is fixed to someone who will remain still, or it is fixed to a heavy piece of equipment. If the explorer gets into trouble, he can be pulled to safety with the line.

34 **flare** (page 26)

a bright light which burns for a short time to light up a large area.

35 **extend** (page 26)

the usual meaning of *extend* is to increase in size in one particular dimension – for example to become longer. It is sometimes used with this meaning in this story. But sometimes *extend* means to occupy all the space between two points. That is the meaning here.

36 **played back** – *to play back* (page 28)

if you record a set of sounds, then play the recording so that other people can hear it, you are *playing it back*.

37 **terrace** (page 29)

a flat, horizontal area which is made in the side of a hill or a curved piece of ground.

38 **concentric** (page 29)

if a number of circles of different sizes have their centres at the same point, these circles are *concentric*.

39 **spike** (page 29)

something which is long and has a point at one end.

40 **factory** (page 30)

a building, or group of buildings, where things are made.

41 **square kilometres** (page 30)
an area which is one kilometre long and one kilometre wide is called one square kilometre.

42 **used up** – *to use up* (page 31)
if you have a fixed amount of something like fuel, energy, air, etc., and you use it all, then your supply of that thing is *used up* and you have *used it up*.

43 **rungs** (page 32)
the horizontal pieces of a ladder, which you put your feet on when you are climbing it.

44 **handrail** (page 33)
a long piece of wood or metal next to, and above, the steps of a stairway. You hold this *handrail* when you are walking on the stairway.

45 **freezing point** (page 33)
the temperature at which a liquid, when cooled, becomes solid. This low temperature is the *freezing point* of that liquid.

46 **thermo-suits** (page 35)
suits of clothes made of a special material which keeps the wearers warm when they are in a very cold place.

47 **in charge** – *to be in charge at a place* (page 36)
if someone controls everything that happens at a particular place, he/she is *in charge* at that place.

48 **sloping** (page 38)
a *slope* is a flat surface, one end of which is higher than the other. This kind of surface can be described as *sloping*.

49 **hammer** (page 39)
a tool which is used for hitting things. A hammer usually has the shape of a letter 'T'.

50 **laser beams** (page 40)
beams of a powerful, special kind of light that can be used to cut hard materials.

51 **sealed** (page 40)
if something is *sealed*, it is closed in a way that stops air, water or anything else getting in or out of it.

52 **hurricanes** (page 41)
violent storms with strong, dangerous winds and heavy rain.

53 **towers and...domes** (page 42)
a *tower* is a building whose height is much greater than its width. A *dome* is a kind of roof for a building. It is the upper half of a sphere.

54 **metallic salts** (page 44)

carbon compounds, phosphates, nitrates and metallic salts are all kinds of chemicals.

55 **artificial environment** (page 54)

a place which is sealed from the atmosphere outside it and which contains an atmosphere which has been specially created for it.

56 **huge resources** (page 54)

large amounts of things which can be used.

57 **rocket propulsion** (page 55)

when something is moved in a particular direction, it is propelled in that direction, and the movement is called propulsion. A spaceship is powered by a rocket motor – a motor which burns fuel so that expanding gases push the ship forward.

58 **gravitational pull** (page 55)

the force created by a large spinning object which pulls things towards its surface. (See page 6.)

59 **moisture** (page 57)

a small amount of liquid – usually water – in the air, in a substance, or on the surface of something.

60 **reacted with** – to react with (page 57)

if two things are brought together and something happens as a result, the two things are reacting with each other. The process is called a reaction.

61 **storage drums** (page 58)

large cylinders which are used to store things.

62 **single-cell life-forms** (page 58)

very simple living things which have only one cell. A cell is the smallest kind of living thing that can exist on its own.

63 **walkways** (page 58)

narrow streets which are raised above the ground.

64 **ramps** (page 59)

sloping surfaces, without steps, which join flat surfaces at higher and lower levels.

65 **sports equipment** (page 61)

everything that you use to play, or take part in, a sport.

66 **propeller** (page 62)

simple kinds of aircraft are moved through the air by a propeller which pulls or pushes them forward. A propeller has blades fixed to a central hub. The propeller spins round and round and moves the air to pull or push the aircraft.

67 **control stick** (page 62)
the *control stick* moves the parts of an aircraft which make it fly through the air, and move it up and down and make it turn.

68 **buttresses** (page 63)
a *buttress* is a piece of wall which is built against a larger wall, to strengthen it.

69 **heart-beat** (page 65)
the sound that your heart makes as it pumps blood round inside your body.

70 **force-field** (page 65)
a *force* is a power which can make an object move, or behave in a particular way. An area in which a force is working is called a *force-field*. These forces, which are invisible, can be electrical, magnetic, gravitational, etc.

71 **parachute** (page 73)
a very large piece of cloth which is joined to a person with strong strings or lines. It slows the speed at which the person falls through the air. People use *parachutes* when they jump from aircraft.

72 **chemistry** (page 78)
here, this word means all the different chemicals which make up an object.

73 **armed missile** (page 83)
a kind of weapon which is powered by rockets. A *missile* is usually a cylinder which has a bomb attached to it.

74 **General Assembly** (page 84)
a meeting of the representatives of all the countries or worlds which make up an organisation like the United Nations today, or the United Planets in this story.

75 **shuttle** (page 88)
a small spaceship which is used for travelling short distances.

76 **antenna** (page 91)
a long thin piece of metal which receives and sends radio signals.

77 **holograms** (page 93)
a *hologram* is a picture of something or someone which looks real and solid. You can look at a hologram from different directions.

78 **harness** (page 93)
a set of strong straps which is fastened round the body of an animal or a person.

Published by Macmillan Heinemann ELT
Between Towns Road, Oxford OX4 3PP
Macmillan Heinemann ELT is an imprint of
Macmillan Publishers Limited
Companies and representatives throughout the world
Heinemann is a registered trademark of Harcourt Education, used under licence.

ISBN 1–405–07303–9
EAN 978–1–405073–03–5

Rendezvous with Rama © Arthur C. Clarke 1973
First published 1973 by Victor Gollancz Limited

Arthur C. Clarke asserts his right to be identified as the author of the
original work *Rendezvous with Rama* of which this Reader is an adaptation.

This retold version by Elizabeth Walker for Macmillan Readers
First published 2003
Text © Macmillan Publishers Limited 2003
Design and illustration © Macmillan Publishers Limited 2003

This edition first published 2005

Designed by Sarah Nicholson
Illustrated by Steve Kyte
Maps and diagrams on pages 7, 10 and 107 by John Gilkes
Cover photograph courtesy of NASA

Printed in Thailand

2009 2008 2007 2006 2005
10 9 8 7 6 5 4 3 2